MINGLING VOICES
Series editor: Manijeh Mannani

Give us wholeness, for we are broken.
But who are we asking, and why do we ask?

— PHYLLIS WEBB

National in scope, *Mingling Voices* draws on the work of both new and established novelists, short story tellers, and poets. The series especially, but not exclusively, aims to promote authors who challenge traditions and cultural stereotypes. It is designed to reach a wide variety of readers, both generalists and specialists. *Mingling Voices* is also open to literary works that delineate the immigrant experience in Canada.

Series Titles

Poems for a Small Park
by E.D. Blodgett

Dreamwork
by Jonathan Locke Hart

Windfall Apples: Tanka and Kyoka
by Richard Stevenson

The dust of just beginning
by Don Kerr

Roy & Me

This Is Not A MEMOIR

BY MAURICE YACOWAR

AU PRESS

© 2010 Maurice Yacowar

Published by AU Press, Athabasca University
1200, 10011 – 109 Street Edmonton, AB T5J 3S8

Library and Archives Canada Cataloguing in Publication

Yacowar, Maurice, 1942–
Roy & me : this is not a memoir / Maurice Yacowar.

(Mingling voices, ISSN 1917-9405)
Also available in electronic format (978-1-926836-11-9).
ISBN 978-1-926836-10-2

1. Yacowar, Maurice, 1942- —Fiction.
2. Farran, Roy, 1921–2006—Fiction.
I. Title.
II. Series: Mingling voices

PS8597.A4R69 2010   c813'.54   c2010-906143-8

Cover and book design by Natalie Olsen, Kisscut Design.
Printed and bound in Canada by Marquis Book Printing.

A volume in the Mingling Voices series:
ISSN 1917-9405 (Print) ISSN 1917-9413 (Online)

*In memory of my son, Sammy,
and my parents, Sam and Sophie Yacowar*

CONTENTS

The difference between opera and life,
I'd noticed, was that in life
one person played all the parts.

LORRIE MOORE, *A Gate at the Stairs*
(New York: Alfred A. Knopf, 2009), p. 317.

# Preface

In the summer of 1958, when I was growing up in
Calgary, I was hired as a cub reporter by the editor
of a local paper, the *North Hill News*. I was a sixteen-
year-old Jewish boy. Although I didn't know it at the
time, the editor, Roy Farran — a British war hero who
would go on to a become a member of the Alberta legislature — was widely suspected of anti-Semitic views
and conduct, including the torture and murder of a
sixteen-year-old Jewish boy in Palestine during the
last days of the British mandate. The scenes that follow recall my relationship with this dashing, enigmatic
man who, apart from my parents, has probably been
the single most influential figure in my life.

That sounds like a memoir, doesn't it? Well, it is and it isn't.

Two stories are juxtaposed here. My remembrances of my early forays into journalism — Roy and his *North Hill News*, along with my adventures as founding editor of my university newspaper — run down the left side of the page. That much is memoir. But over on the right side is the kind of shameless fantasy that has no place in a self-respecting memoir. There I compose a Roy Farran out of other material — his novels, his memoirs (sometimes drawing on his words, sometimes using my own). The notes acknowledge my use of Farran's published writings, which I habitually paraphrase. Thanks to my flypaper memory, in the conversations I recall, I quote him verbatim — his voice filtered, of course, through five decades of dead flies. Other scenes and speeches are entirely my invention. On his role in the Jewish boy's murder, I've also drawn on David Cesarani's revelations in *Major Farran's Hat: Murder, Scandal and Britain's War Against Jewish Terrorism, 1945–1948*.[1]

Given Roy's politics, there's a certain poetic justice in that allocation of space — my story on the left, Roy's to the right. But I'm looking for another kind of justice. I'm trying to weigh the conflicting aspects of that remarkable man's life, if only to renegotiate what he meant to me and how he influences me still. Nor should we forget the sixteen-year-old Jewish boy whom Roy apparently killed — Alexander Rubovitz. His voice still needs to be heard.

Of course there is no balance to the page thus divided. I may have more words than Roy has now, but my life is a Popsicle-stick raft beside his Hokusai wave. And the young Alexander Rubovitz has the fewest words, the shortest life, yet he casts the heaviest shadow.

So on the left is my memory, on the right my fancy. But even memory refracts through the prism of imagination. I wonder whether any memoir can be entirely free of fantasy. For even what I am confident is an accurate memory may still harbour traces of subjective intervention. We are all stuck in our own perspective. Often our memory skews to what we'd like things to have been. Like our favourite mirror, our hindsight flatters us, or we prefer the funhouse distortion that catches our fears. Conversely, our imagination is fueled by what's real. Here my fantasy of Roy draws more on what I've been reading than on what I may have been smoking. Here each story, as well as the collision of the two, moves between those conventionally discrete poles: history and fiction. So this is not a memoir — or, rather, it is more than that. It's an experiment in the genre, one that not only admits but exercises the subjectivity in our memories.

In approaching this work, the reader is requested to set aside any usual expectations of a history, a novel, a psychoanalytic study, a confession. As its slender heft may suggest, what follows is more akin to the classical closet drama. In the three hours' traffic of the page, the interplaying voices — two main ones, a few supporting characters — address themes of memory, ambition and guilt, relationships and their influence, and responsibilities and how we rationalize them. Above all, the interwoven narratives explore an accident of history, in which an ordinary small life happened to engage with one much larger. For we are all living in some history — and who knows how many fictions. Finally, as in live theatre more than in prose fiction, the themes speak to the moment of performance as much as to the moment of the setting. The them, there, are also the us, now.

This work grew out of a short article on Farran, "Double Life," published in the June 2009 issue of *Alberta Views* (pp. 37–39). The present title fought off a spirited challenge from *Roy and I*. My two main characters are the object — not the agent — of my creative recollection.

✳ ✳ ✳

The author expresses his heartiest gratitude to Walter Hildebrandt for his understanding and encouragement, to Pamela Holway for her dedicated, constructive editing far beyond the call of duty, and to Natalie Olsen for a book and cover design that can only be called inspired. To my wife, Anne Petrie, my usual love and special thanks for suggesting this project and for unreservedly supporting me here as in all else.

Roy & Me

I was in London when Roy Farran died. "Shit," I said, when on my return I heard the news. "I missed his bloody funeral."

I'd been looking forward to it. Not that I wished to see him dead; I just wanted to say hello to a few of the living. I hadn't seen the guys from the *North Hill News* for some fifty years. Like the crew from the print shop, foreman Milt Knight, his successor, Dick, the pressman, Frank, the linotype operator, George Volk. No, he's dead, his wife told me, a wonderful, funny man taken tragically young. But his brother, Bill, is still alive. Then there was young Billy, who would bellow "Mule Skinner Blues" ("Good mornin' cap-*tain*") to punctuate the boredom. Bill MacCallum is gone too. He did the leg work to start the Calgary Winter Club. Limp and all. There's a legacy for you.

Now Graham Smith, who took over from Roy as editor, he has just passed away too. And the soon-to-be cartoonist Ben Wicks, who briefly worked in the print shop when he first alit from England.[2] He'd been referred to Roy as a key figure in the expatriate British community here. Ben's gone. This "Going, going, gone" motif is sadly unrelated to auctions.

I looked up the report in the *Calgary Herald*. Dead at 85, Roy Alexander St. Thomas Farran.

Alexander? Yes, Alexander. And St. Thomas.

I'd only heard him called "Roy," and I only spoke to "Mr. Farran." If I call him "Roy" now, it's because I'm sixty-eight and he's gone altogether. Well, out of earshot.

Quite a funeral I missed, too. Soldiers from the Strathcona Regiment came from all over to give Roy an artillery salute. That's rare. A procession ten blocks long slow-marched from Saint Anthony's Church to the McInnis & Holloway Funeral Home. Calgary had never seen that before. Military representatives came from France, Greece, Italy.

Roy's military record allowed nothing less. He was one of the most highly decorated soldiers in World War II: Distinguished Service Order, Military Cross (twice), stars for the Africa, France-Germany, and Italy campaigns, Queen's Gold and Silver Jubilee medals, both Officier and Chevalier de la Légion d'honneur, American Legion of Merit, Italian Medaglia d'Oro and Partisan Star of the Garibaldi, Greek War Medal, and the French Croix de Guerre with Palm. All those medals. Had he been Jewish, he could've opened a pawn shop.

A genuine war hero. And ... *I* knew him. For a while there, I would say I idolized him. And now I'm left to wonder.

* * *

My high school principal, Mr. (a.k.a. Gordon A.) Foster, gave me permission to take an afternoon off from school for my job interview.

The *North Hill News* was at 310 16th Avenue NW. Today, the building, now sandwiched between a Vietnamese and a sushi restaurant, houses an equipment rental outfit, a mortgage company, and a tattoo parlour. Publishing has changed.

I pretended confidence when the receptionist pointed me to the first office on the left. I strode down the hall as if someone were watching.

"Mr. Farran?" I offered from the doorway.

"Yes?"

"I'm Maurice Yacowar? The lady in the front said I should come through? We have an appointment?"

"Of course. Come in. Take that seat."

There were two desks in the room, at a 90-degree angle, each sheltering a wooden armchair. Mr. Farran sat in one; I took the one on the right. A Calgary street map was the only item on the walls.

Roy was a very handsome man. He had a full head of silver hair, a firm jaw, an aquiline nose, a clear, ruddy complexion, and a husky, solid build that his striped suspenders failed to demean. He usually spoke with a chuckle, but over the years I would see that he could also flash steel.

"I have your letter here," he rummaged. "Somewhere. If you're going to be a journalist, you will have to learn to master mess. Aaah. So, it's Morris . . . how do you pronounce the rest?"

"*Yac*-owar. Maur-*ice Yac*-owar. My father's from Odessa so it was originally Ya-*kov*-er. It was anglicized to Yacowar."

I didn't say *we* anglicized it. Everyone covers *some* tracks, passes *some* buck. If that omission was a lie, it was little and white.

"You're sixteen. But with previous employment! Usher at the Hitchin' Post, one year now. How is that going?"

"Well, I've always liked movies, especially Westerns. But last weekend I got to watch *Storm over the Nile* six times. Excellent film. Do you know it? With Laurence Harvey?"

"The remake of *The Four Feathers?* A fine book. I believe there was an earlier film version, with Ralph Richardson."

"Could be. The job is good, but East Calgary's a bit

rough. I had to lie about my age, but I need that 60 cents an hour."

"Do you wear the blue uniform?"

"Yes, sir. It's very itchy. My chemistry lab partner, John, he ushers at the Capital.[3] He says his suit doesn't itch."

"So even here there's a class system, what?" That ready chuckle.

"I guess. Anyway, now I'm sixteen and legal, I thought I'd try for a real job? I've always wanted to be a writer."

"Here's your first lesson. You can't be a *writer* on a newspaper. There's no room for flowery prose. Get down the facts. Like *Dragnet*. You're writing for a thin column on the page so you can't run on. You need discipline. Precision."

"That's good to know, sir."

"Do you type?"

"Not very fast." I demonstrated with two fingers in the air. I probably managed a typo even there.

"You don't want to type faster than you think. That's like a soldier who shoots before he sees. What are your career plans?"

"I'm going to UAC in September." At that time, the "University of Calgary" consisted of the University of Alberta's Calgary branch, housed in a wing at the Southern Alberta Institute of Technology (known locally as "the Tech"). "I'll major in English, then do either journalism or law. Maybe do a minor in commerce, so I could go into corporate law."

"That sounds sensible. I see you've edited school papers. Grade Nine. Grade Eleven. The yearbook. Oh yes, your Sputnik editorial." The *Herald*, Calgary's afternoon daily, had reprinted my school paper piece on their editorial page. I had subtly included a copy in my application.

"To be frank, I find it a bit overwritten. Purple prose will see you through school but not here. Still, you're off to not a bad start. Why didn't you apply to the *Herald?*"

"I did, sir. And *The Albertan*. You were the only one who replied."

Roy smiled: "I appreciate your honesty. It says here you're Jewish."

"Yes, sir. I'm president of the Jewish fraternity this year. The AZA. That doesn't do much for my writing, but it gives me experience in public speaking."

"Yes. Well, Morris, that was a very good letter. It was . . . complete. I suppose I could use some help. Oh, you're at Central, not Crescent Heights. You live on the south side?"

"Yes, on 36th Avenue at 11th. But I can bus here early every morning. Just one change, at The Bay."

"Around nine is fine, when the phone calls start. But journalists don't punch clocks. Some days you leave

early; some days you work late. More often the latter. As it happens I live in Mount Royal, on Hillcrest
Avenue. We're closer than you'd think."

* * *

My parents were newly arrived to Mount Royal. More
precisely, to South Mount Royal, where newer bun-
galows wafted behind the established mansions like
the Farrans'.

As Roy explained, the paper's mandate was everything north of the river. It delivered local news, nothing
earth-shaking, just family and neighborhood stories,
along with whatever City Council business affected
the north side.

The *North Hill News* was delivered free on Thurs-
days to every front door in the area. On Tuesdays Roy
published a farm paper on contract for the Rocky View
municipality. Public notices, farm news, the latest
market prices. Both papers depended on advertising
for revenue.

The company also did job printing, which ranged
from political flyers and wedding invitations to subcon-
tracted work for the *High River Times*. The publisher's
son, Joe Clark, occasionally drove into Calgary from
High River (a town not far south) to drop jobs off or
pick them up. I'd see him streak past the office to the
print shop, then out again. He'd occasionally pause for

badinage with Roy. Joe and I didn't talk till university.[4]

I would work on both papers, edit submissions, such as wedding reports, do some reporting, proof the galleys, handle calls. Basically, Roy would write the editorial page, and I would come to do everything else.

"We'll start you on our usual apprentice salary, $19.76 a week after deductions. That's what we pay in our print shop. How does that sound?"

"Fine, sir. When do I start?"

"How's the second of July?"

"Sure."

"You can start with some work around here, to learn the ropes. Then I'll send you down to the Stampede. We're like the dailies during the Stampede: all eyes are on it. The rest of the year we focus on neighbourhood stories. Come, I'll show you around. You've met Doreen out front. You'll meet my partner, Bill MacCallum, next time. He handles the business end. Here, I'll introduce you to the lads in the print shop. You'll enjoy them."

I was a newspaper man.

He seems a level-headed lad. I'll give him odd jobs. Two months. If he doesn't pan out, we shan't have him back next year. I have nothing to lose.

Sixteen. But Jewish sixteen-year-olds are older. They're men at thirteen. At least that's their rite of passage, the bar mitzvah. Not like the bar for *our* rites of manhood, I'll wager.

You don't find those Jewish boys drunk. Man or boy, don't think I ever saw a Jew drunk in my life. I've flown with them, too.

No, wait. That's a myth. Come to think, I have seen a few fair sheets to the wind. Beware of the stereotype, even the positive ones.

Sixteen. That boy was sixteen. Rubovitch. Rubovitz. Alexander Rubovitz. Sixteen. I hear there's a street named after him in Jerusalem. In East Talpiot, I think.

They never did find his body. They bloody well found my hat, but not his body. At least, they said it was my hat. The name on the hatband was a tad hard to read.

A trilby it was. Quite dashing.

1947. It was May 6th. The boy was putting up posters for those Jewish terrorists. The Stern Gang. The Jews insisted he was abducted, tied to a tree, stripped and tortured to death. Then, supposedly, his corpse was stabbed repeatedly, so that the blood would draw the jackals, to drag him off for dinner. That was their story. They never dropped it. They made a huge fuss about the incident.

They never found his body.

But I was in the clear. I had my alibi. All that evening I was undercover at a dinner, in disguise as an Arab. I was in another part of Jerusalem altogether. In Givat Shaul, as a matter of fact.

The witnesses to the Jewish lad's abduction, they said they saw a man with a gun force him into a car. But they couldn't pick me out of a lineup. As for my hat, I explained that I'd lent it to someone. That it was planted there to frame me.

But the Jews wouldn't let go. They fingered me. At the time I was Deputy Superintendent of Police. A prime target.[5]

The procedure was simple. I typed my copy on 6"x 8" precut newsprint, to fit the slot on the old linotype machine. On the top right corner I'd type the title, then, say, "p. 1 of 4," and at the end finish with the professional flourish: "— 30 —." Whatever that meant. Didn't ask, didn't know, just did.

Roy and I worked in the one real office. Bill Mac-Callum and Dorothy MacDonald, a sprightly married woman in advertising, shared a small space off the receptionist's in the front. There were two washrooms in the hallway — ladies first — then the large printing shop in the back. From the print shop, it was guys first, come to think of it.

At the time, I didn't know anything about Roy or his background. But I liked the fact that he was British. I was already an Anglophile, equally devoted to English literature and British film comedies. Indeed, if my film-teaching career began with that itchy blue suit at the Hitchin' Post, from my love of British comedy sprang my ardor for Shakespeare — including my doctoral studies at the Shakespeare Institute in Birmingham (UK, as I used to say, where the race riots were, though they paled beside those in Alabama). My dissertation —"John Lyly and the Uses of Irony"— grew out of my fascination with British pop culture and the mingling of brows high and low.

I had watched George Formby movies and coaxed

my mother into taking me to a Tommy Trinder concert at the Palace. I faithfully attended the *St. Trinian's, Doctor in the House,* and *Carry On* films when they cropped up at the Plaza, the Tivoli, or — infrequently — the Marda, where *Genevieve* ran for a year. That was when the Marda was a cinema, not the gentrified Marda Loop. Until I discovered the Goons, *Take It from Here* and *Round the Horne* were my favourite radio programs, right up there with Wayne and Schuster and *Lux Presents Hollywood*.

One *St. Trinian's* film opened with the school ablaze. "There's always trouble when there's arson around," the narrator intoned. Nobody else in the Plaza audience, I was pleased to note, laughed. And in the first *Doctor in the House*:

"Two big breaths."

"Yeth, and I'm only thickthteen."

Clearly, the Brits gave me my sophisticated sense of humour.

＊ ＊ ＊

After my first paper was put to bed, Roy and I skimmed the issue.

"Satisfying, what? Your piece on the two-headed calf was very good. You struck a good light tone there."

"Oh, thanks. I enjoyed looking around the grounds. The press pass sure makes a difference."

"But you must be an old hand at the Stampede."

"Not really. I grew up in a rooming house on the corner of 12th Avenue and 3rd Street East. Five blocks from the stockade. My mum took my sister and me on Family Day but mainly to collect pop and beer bottles. Our spending money. We'd watch the fireworks from our backyard."

I didn't tell him that in the early fifties we would set up cots in the halls of our rooming house to rent for three dollars a night. Once we even rented out my sister's bedroom, which was curtained off from our kitchen. I slept on our dining room chairs, aligned in two rows of three. Calgary did not have the hotels it has now.

* * *

I'd screw up.

"Dammit, Morris. Here! You've misspelled Passchendaele."

"Sorry."

"I thought you were a good student. Didn't you do history?"

"We only did Canadian."

"That's not good enough. And here. A trophy 'emblematic of supremacy.' That's a cliché. If you've heard a phrase twice before, don't use it. All right?"

"Yes, sir."

The army suppressed its report on Rubovitz's disappearance for over a month. Not for my sake, no. They'd found some names on him, which they were investigating. They didn't want to scare the new suspects off.

Suddenly I heard the army was going to charge *me* with his murder.

You see, a UN commission was coming over, and the unsolved murder made Britain seem unable to rule Palestine any more. That's what the Jews wanted. To hasten our departure. Trying me for murder would shine up the British government's image.

I needed time to talk some sense into them, don't you see?

A couple of my men stole a Ford V8 and spirited me off to Syria. I had no papers, just a stash of, oh, maybe a hundred pounds. By now the whole world knew I was wanted for murder. The world press had pounced on the story of Rubovitz's disappearance, and they all in lockstep blamed me.

That Ford could leave in the dust anything they'd send after me.

The British government — right up to the PMO — were hugely embarrassed that I hadn't already been arrested. They tried to extradite me. Instead the Syrians offered me political asylum. They said they would make me a colonel if I would train their troops in guerrilla warfare.

I certainly considered the offer.

I've always liked the Arabs. They are the most generous, hospitable people on earth. Your typical Arab, even though hc is disdained by the world, he's rather like a Connemara peasant. He has that simple dignity. Their women are less promiscuous than ours, their men less worldly, less ambitious.

True, their sanitation left much to be desired. But their primitive toilet is no reason for foreigners to steal an Arab's land.[6]

Now, I wasn't anti-Semitic. Most certainly not. I just felt for the Arabs, who were unfairly despised for their lack of sophistication and their colour.

But for me to live in Syria and help their cause? No.

I could not bear the thought that I might ever cause British deaths. Even indirectly. I would rather become a martyr for Britain than do that.

After securing certain assurances, I surrendered to the British Consul in Damascus.

I'd stolen ten days of freedom. Now I would stand trial in Jerusalem.

Roy put down the new issue. "So, Morris, tell me about yourself. What does your father do?"

"Nothing now. He used to ranch in Saskatchewan. He's still very good with his hands. You know, fixing things, plumbing, carpentry. But he got septicemia from a coyote. Blood poisoning. He's been allergic to animals ever since. And with his asthma, he hasn't been able to work for years. That's why we moved to that rooming house. We moved here from Leader, Saskatchewan, in August 1950. In time for school. Sometimes my mum gets work as a substitute teacher, but mainly she's home looking after my dad. She gives him his needles."

I didn't mention our excitement when Dad once got a job selling shoes at The Bay. The good times would begin. Maybe I could get barber shop haircuts instead of with Mum's nipping clippers. Halfway through his first day he was sent home. An asthma attack had scared the hell out of the customers. They thought he was dying.

"You should feel at home on the farm paper then."

"Not really. I have no memories from the ranch. Just from Leader. I'm a city boy."

"Well, next week I'll send you out to the country. Better bring an old pair of shoes. The muck, you know. You might want to keep an old pair here. But downwind from me. I should have asked, do you drive? You have a licence?"

"Yes, but no car."

"You can take mine. That yellow Buick on Second Street. It's a company car. Just don't turn hot-rodder on me, what?"

"I wouldn't."

"Of course not. Your parents, how do they feel about your working . . . here?"

"They're tickled pink. Mum always encouraged my reading and writing. Dad, he taught himself to read. When he came over in 1912, he joined the Canadian army to learn English. So when he sees me making money with words . . . well, I'm doing what he struggled for."

"They must be very proud of you."

"They're just relieved I'm not a juvenile delinquent."

"You've been doing very well. Look, you needn't run your copy past me any more. Just keep that *Chambers* close to hand. Write, edit, then run it out to George on the linotype. Of course, if you want, you can always check anything with me. Otherwise you're on your own."

My dad in the army. On the government records website I recently found his army papers, his registration, and the stamp showing his release. Everything fits except he's identified as a Lutheran. He planned to homestead after the army; perhaps he feared Jews wouldn't be given land. Anyway, the official records have him a Lutheran. Records.

Our police betrayed me. During my trial, instead of focusing on the two witnesses to the abduction who could *not* identify me, they suggested others did. I could see where we were headed. I was in trouble.

When I went to dinner with my guard, I gave him the slip. Skipped out through the loo window. I'd managed to get a message through to a Bedouin friend, who was waiting. He helped me across Transjordan to the Saudi border. I was safe.

I would have stayed there, quite content. But those bloody Jewish terrorists, they vowed reprisal for my escape.

They killed four soldiers sunning on the beach in Tel Aviv. They seriously wounded my dear friend John Waddie when they shot up the Astoria Restaurant. Then they killed my friend Kissane in Haifa. That settled it.

I made it back on my own and on a bright June morning surrendered myself at the Allenby Barracks gate. I would stand trial.

I knew I might well be hanged. But if that's how Britain needed me to serve her, I was willing.[7]

I had a flair for real estate fluff. For Mr. MacCallum's special sections launching a new subdivision, I poured out the celebratory prose. Perhaps this talent reflected my modest experience with real estate, with my parents' rooming house and the few other rental properties they had added over the years. More likely, though, it was just my joy at stringing out words — of whatever function.

I served a special interest when I had to fill a few columns for the opening of Phil's Pancake House next door. The owner was an energetic Mr. Cohen, whose name was not, in fact, Phil and for whose daughter, Carole, I had long harboured a shy case of the hots. When I heard that Carole's kid brother was systematically eating his way through the entire menu, I thought I could score some points with the family. I'd make her brother a celebrity.

I shot a Polaroid of the kid and wrote a short piece on his favourite dishes and the progress of his campaign to date. I led off with stats on the menu's range and then segued into the kid's project with, "But Phil's pancakes can be beat." I meant, of course, that the vast and diverse menu could, like Everest, be conquered.

When the paper appeared, instead of appreciating my salute to the corpulent fruit of his loins, Mr. Cohen stormed in: "What the hell is this? You should have said 'Phil's pancakes *can't* be beat'! What's the matter with you?"

Alas, I learned, not everyone appreciates the importance of context.

When I was awaiting court martial at Allenby Barracks in Jerusalem, there was a distinct possibility that the Zionist terrorists would take justice into their own hand and try to lift me. I was put under the guard of 55th Field Squadron, Royal Engineers, at Ramallah.

I was working late one day when Roy returned from a long City Council meeting.

"Any calls?"

"Nothing important. A lot of people are upset about that cement comment in your Chatterbox column."

Roy had enigmatically written: "What city father paved his home driveway with city cement?"

"As well they should be. The fur sure flew at Council. Some aldermen threatened legal action if I don't retract."

"What are you going to do?"

Roy smiled impishly: "Well, they appear to be forcing my hand. Plain and simple. Thursday's lead will identify the culprit."

"Who is it?"

"Will you keep it secret till Thursday?"

"I won't tell a soul."

"It's our beloved Mayor Don Mackay."

"Mayor Mackay? But he's so popular."

"He's also a glad-handing, supercilious, corrupt twit. The City of Calgary deserves better."

That's how it began, the paper's campaign to unseat the mayor. Every issue had a new attack. Roy did all the writing on this, in high dudgeon against political corruption. The paper's motto —"Without Fear or Favour"— he really meant it.

Roy's rhetoric was so heated that some people cancelled their subscriptions. Of course, the paper was free, so they didn't have subscriptions. But they'd call to cancel them anyway.

The controversy soon spread throughout the city.

———

At my court martial I was acquitted. Of course I was acquitted. Well, the official verdict was: "No case to answer." There was a little circumstantial evidence but nobody and nothing to link me directly to the crime. Just a lot of political anger. But I was acquitted. That was October 2nd, 1947.

My guards, the Royal Engineers, could now leave Palestine. When their commanding officer, Major Richard Clutterbuck, announced my acquittal while the company was on parade, there was an explosion of loud cheers. However black the situation would become, I was always heartened by the support of my troops. They knew me.

Roy came in as I was lighting up my new pipe.

Now, understand, my pipe was not a pipe. It was an image — not of a pipe but of a different me. An older, more sophisticated, more experienced, dare I say more suave me, an image only a sixteen-year-old could trick himself into believing.

"Good morning, Morris. Here, there's a rumour that the police were called out to the mayor's home last week. Some threatening stranger on his doorstep. May have had a gun. Nobody will talk about it. See if you can find out whether it's true."

"Good."

"Say, what's that you're smoking?"

"Mixture #79. A friend put me onto it."

"It smells like a Turkish bordello. Here, try some of this. It's Amphora. They have different colours for their different aromas, but I like the Brown. It's pure."

I switched tobacco. Amphora at work (Brown, of course) and Mixture #79 on dates — till I'd used it up.

In addition to the pipe, I already wore a business uniform of brown sport jacket, brown slacks, tie, and straw hat. I felt like Cary Grant in *His Girl Friday*. Nonetheless I had not scored even a single date with a North Hill girl.

I came up with a plan to find out about the police call to Mackay's house. It may have been a tad self-serving, but it was a plan.

Mayor Mackay's oldest daughter, Donna, was captain of the Crescent Heights High School cheer-leaders. I would phone her to propose a series of personal pieces about the girls on her team, starting with her. If she agreed, would she please get me their photos and phone numbers for my interviews? Then I would nonchalantly ask her about the rumour. A date with Donna or one of her girls would be my not-unwarranted bonus for discovering the truth behind the rumour.

I called Donna from home that evening. She was receptive but said she'd have to check with her school advisor. She didn't think there would be a problem, though, so we proceeded with her interview.

"Do you play any sports yourself? . . . What do you do on weekends? Do you like movies? . . . Uh, huh . . . Are you going steady? . . . What's his name? . . . Is he at

Crescent too? ... Where does he work? ... Well, I guess that covers it for me. Is there anything you'd like to add? ... Oh, not at all, I've really enjoyed talking to you. I think cheerleaders deserve as much attention as athletes, don't you? ... When can I get the pictures and phone numbers? ... Maybe we could meet for dinner? ... No, a root beer's fine. 4:30 Tuesday, A&W on 16th. Tuesday will get you into next week's paper. By the way, that must have been quite a scare, that stranger at your front door. ... Yeah. ... Wow. ... When was it, exactly? ... Well, I can imagine. ... Politics, some people just go too far. ... You're really brave. ... Let's hope so. ... Me too. Look forward to seeing you. Tuesday, 4:30, A&W on 16th. ... Bye. And thanks."

I felt a shade guilty about tricking Donna Mackay. But it worked. It gave us a three-line scoop in Roy's Chatterbox column. When we met, she didn't appear mad that I'd tricked her into confirming the rumour. Maybe she didn't realize. And the story was a nothing — just a perturbed, unarmed citizen wanting a word with the mayor.

Mr. Farran approved.

"Your Donna Mackay story was very good. We've had several calls to restart subscriptions. They said they'd cancelled because of what they called our personal vendetta against the mayor. But our kindness towards his daughter has won them back. Keep on those cheerleaders. You might even get a girlfriend out of it, what? Don't be shy."

I must have blushed at his joke, but that was my hope. Still, I didn't ask Donna out, or any of her girls. I would have needed Roy's company car for the date, and he always drove it home.

More generally, the verdict on my court martial was not so well received.

Even though the body had not been found, the police had told the Rubovitz family that their son was dead. They didn't say how.

The Jews plastered the walls with libellous pictures of me. The Jewish officials, the Jewish press, they were furious — about the delay in my arrest, about what they called the secrecy of the trial, and now of course the verdict. The international press fell into step. Suddenly I was supposed to hate Jews.

That's balderdash. My driver in France in '44 was a Polish Jew. Kalkstein. When he was killed I had him buried in a churchyard. In Recey-sur-

Ource. Full military honours. You see, I respected him.[8]

And Lieutenant Stephens, an Austrian Jew. I requested him specifically, to serve as a translator for us on Operation Tombola.[9]

That Palestinian, George Filar — he was a Jew, and a damned brave chap to boot. He led a group of Jewish prisoners through a sewer out of the Corinth prison camp. He also helped four New Zealanders escape from Kokinia.

I flew with a few, too. Always professional, effective, sober.

And the women in the *kibbutzim*. Beauties. Perfect creatures, bronzed, muscular, gutsy. How they turned the desert into a garden is miraculous. True, some were big-arsed, but there were beauties too.

Tel Aviv put most Middle East cities to shame. But then I came to see its underbelly. For all its idealism, it adopted the worst of American consumerism. The prostitutes. Fat, cigar-smoking business kings perched like vultures at the top. And Orthodox boys, with their ringlets and hanging threads — but carrying bombs in their pockets. Those Jewish terrorists, they had no scruples.[10]

Now, one thing's true. I have said that the Jews may be responsible for the rise in anti-Semitism. But I was referring to their terrorist attacks on civilians. That hardly makes me anti-Semitic. Anti-Jewish-terrorist, yes, which any reasonable man must be. Why, even President Nixon, Billy Graham, they have said it: Jews can provoke anti-Semitism.

Roy's campaign against the mayor led to heated debates in City Council. I remember Alderman James Macdonald: "You can't be half pregnant!" he said, when some councilors tried to minimize the mayor's corruption. Macdonald resigned from Council and decamped to the West Indies.

"Yes, Morris," Roy said, "Macdonald is a good man. He has principles. But don't forget, he's removing himself, on principle, to a tax haven."

Roy taught me to read beneath the surface.

Mayor Mackay told City Council he had intended to pay for the cement but had just forgotten. No crime in that. But a judicial investigation uncovered a pattern of gifts from companies that had business dealings with the city. In 1959, for the first time in his career, Mackay lost an election.[11]

This modern age. It's not that it has lost its values. It has lost the courage, the will, to make a judgement. People today, they've learned to argue truth, to find two sides to any issue. But they're afraid to make a judgement. They're afraid to offend. To them, everything is in grey. They've forgotten that there is a black, there is a white, especially in morality. Think the way they've been raised to think and you lose your will to survive. Had we thought like that, we would all be under Hitler's boot.[12]

I was proud of Mr. Farran and proud to be working for him. So I was jolted to hear complaints about him from the Calgary Jewish community. As one elderly Jew reproached my parents:

"Your son, a smart boy, vy should he vork for such an antee-Semeet? Vot's wrong mit *De Albertan?* Dis Farran, you know, he blames de Jews for anti-Semitism. You know da sonofabitch killed a Jewish boy? Got away with it, da bastid."

A visiting Jewish official approached me directly:

"Moishe, you did an excellent job on that Israel Bond Drive newspaper. Your AZA chapter gets the official credit, but we know — you and your friend Joel Horwitz did all the work. But let me tell you something, I hope you won't be offended. This Mr. Roy Farran you're working for, you know there's a price on his head in Israel? There's people who would sweep him off to Israel to stand trial. Just like Eichmann. If you could say where he was planning to be some night, there could be a reward. Maybe four thousand dollars?"

One of my sister Ruthie's dates asked her:

"Is it true your brother is working for that Roy Farran? He's terrible. You know there's a character in *Exodus* based on him? A mean British officer. So what's your brother up to anyway?"

My answer was always the same. Roy Farran is a good man, a devout Catholic, a devoted public servant. If he was ever anti-Semitic, I haven't seen any sign of it. He treats me well, and he's teaching me a lot.

Privately I was actually — as the British say — quite

chuffed. Roy Farran was the only fictional character I knew in real life.

Palestine was a snakepit.

Back in November 1917, Foreign Secretary Arthur Balfour committed Britain to establishing in Palestine a national home for the Jews. So the plan was in place well before the Holocaust. That is often forgotten now.

In 1922 the League of Nations gave Britain the mandate to establish the new country of Israel in the area west of the River Jordan. That only increased the Arabs' anxiety and anger. Especially when Jewish immigrants began to flood in for refuge from the Nazis.

The Jews refused to live under an antagonistic Arab majority, and the Arabs wouldn't have anything else. Not much has changed, what?

The British forces were caught in the crossfire, of course — with the Jews now further determined to drive Britain out of their "homeland."

In fact, even though the organization had been outlawed, our government coddled the Haganah because they were less bloody than the Stern Gang. The Haganah only wanted more Jewish immigration and a limited Jewish state. That made them moderates. The radicals like the Stern Gang wanted an Israel that included even Turkish Syria.

Stern himself, the radical the terrorists named themselves after, he was a lunatic bastard. He actually put out feelers offering to fight with the Arabs and the Nazis, just to kill the British. Remember, he was a Jew, but he offered to fight *with* the Nazis.

The Stern Gang was made up of some five hundred nihilists whom even the Jews claimed to reject. They murdered six parachutists as they sat in a tent in Tel Aviv, just writing letters home. Add seven thousand Irgun, another right-wing bunch of Revisionist radicals, with their own network of cells, and we were in trouble.

The terrorists were fired up by what

they said was our foot-dragging on our promise to create a Jewish state. They didn't believe we would do it on our own, so they turned up the pressure.

Of course, one of the Irgun leaders was Menachem Begin, who went on to become an Israeli prime minister. It's the old story. Win the war and your "terrorist" becomes a "freedom fighter."

As they say, the survivor gets to write the history. *Caveat lector.*

Roy kept fighting. He used the paper to mount a campaign against public fluoridation, running grisly photos of rotted teeth and cancerous mouths. As a staunch libertarian, he opposed any form of mass medication. To him fluoride was Huxley's soma.

I did not agree with his sensationalist rhetoric. Some of his pictures and arguments were excessive. But that's the British tabloid style. It apparently worked.

I didn't argue.

* * *

"Here's an evening job for you, Morris, but only if you want it. Reginald Maudling is in town for a social evening with the British community here. Fundraising, really. He's contending for the Tory leadership. I've arranged for you to meet with him privately for twenty minutes on Wednesday night. That's if you'd like. It's not a story the paper needs, but you might want the experience."

"I sure would. Thanks."

The interview came off well, once I got over all the black suits and fancy dresses at the host's Mount Royal mansion. It was even grander than Roy's. After that, of course, I rooted for Maudling to become prime minister. I no longer remember, but I dearly hope that visions of an ambassadorship didn't dance in my modest head.

✳ ✳ ✳

"Why don't you go over to the Tech campus, the university side, and interview Andrew Doucette? He's an old school principal, but he's been working like blazes to get a real university going here. Before they turn him out to pasture, why don't you tap his ideas? You'll be going to UAC, so it won't hurt to meet him."

✳ ✳ ✳

"A football column? Why not? Our readers are interested in the Stampeders. Gridiron Gossip, good title. Mind, it's on your own time. Don't look for any release for it. But if a column will get you into Mewata Stadium for the games, fine."

It did. Sort of. In my capacity as AZA president, I had met Jim Finks, who had come up for one last run as quarterback before taking over as the Stampeders' general manager.[13] I'd invited him to address one of our Sunday evening meetings. When I called him in my new role as football columnist, he didn't remember me, but he advised me that to get into the Mewata press box I would need permission from the senior reporter, *Herald* sports editor Gorde Hunter.

As it happened, I'd also met Hunter through an AZA booking. That had led to my brief stint covering stock car races for the *Herald*, a task considerably complicated by my want of wheels. But, wary of freeloaders (the nerve of some people!), Hunter refused to let the *North Hill News* football editor into the Mewata Stadium's press box. So I had to cadge a ticket from Mr. Finks.

Even newspapers, I discovered, have a class system.

When I finally moved back to Calgary, after thirty years away, I immediately did two things: (1) bought a plot in the Jewish cemetery, the original, the first edition; and (2) bought Stampeder season tickets.

The Stern Gang set off an explosion in the British Embassy in Rome. They blew up our army's headquarters in the King David Hotel in Jerusalem. About a hundred dead. They blew up the British Colonial Club off Trafalgar Square.

Our government reacted weakly, so the attacks grew more violent. We played catch-and-release with those bloody-minded, self-righteous bastards.

As for all the "moderate" Jews who disavowed the extremists, we never got inside info from them, or warnings, or follow-ups. The terrorists always evaporated into their communities. With our British devotion to compromise and manners, we played right into the killers' hands. What we saw as being "reasonable" the terrorists took as being soft. Playing soft with terrorists only emboldens them.

Frankly I was relieved when I was called back to lecture at Sandhurst. I didn't know as much as I pretended, but it was good fun. I remember boning up on some rudimentary guide to bookkeeping the night before holding forth on the subject to my class.

But my teaching career was short-lived. I was recalled to Palestine when the police there proved hopeless, even under army control.

The War Office put Bernard Fergusson, who had trained me when I was a cadet at Sandhurst, in charge of anti-terrorist activities. He assigned me one of his two commando units, to roust the Jewish underground.

We had carte blanche.

I wore the blue Palestine police uniform when I landed at Lydda — it was St Patrick's Day — but never again. We would always set forth dressed as *kibbutzniks* — their shirts, trousers, grey caps or Panamas. We sniffed for leads, tailed suspects, attacked where we saw danger.

It was a touchy business. We were fighting civilian warriors, but we had to avoid injuring innocent civilians.

Still, we had carte blanche.[14]

At one unexpected aspect of the job I proved an abject failure.

Mr. Farran had been hiring a well-known photographer, Walter Petrigo, to take pictures for the paper. To save money, he suggested that I could cover a story and shoot it too.

Good theory, but it didn't work out. I could handle head shots with the Polaroid alright. That camera was foolproof. But the fancy flash camera stymied me.

The first thing Roy showed me was how to insert the bulb. "At an angle," he said, "like an excited man." I'm sure I blushed. Perhaps it was my embarrassment at the joke that rendered my efforts at photography impotent.

Nothing came out right. Ever. Sometimes I suspected that Petrigo, who was still paid to develop the film, was sabotaging my work in order to recover his shooting assignments. In any case, I was a failure as a photographer.

That said, I can claim three photographic successes.

The first was a happy accident. Roy sent me to Riley Park to shoot the Sunday afternoon cricket match. Forgetting to advance the film resulted in a triple exposure, which caught three separate moments of play in one frame. Roy ran it as a poetic image.

The second came as part of our response to complaints about a man who lived in a shack full of animals, with a junk-filled yard as unkempt as he was. The neighbours who called hoped that an exposé would result in his eviction. But as I heard and wrote the story, what emerged was a sad man suffering through a life of loss and forced solitude, his love for his animals, and the alienation of a rural spirit trapped in the strictures of town. His vigilant neighbours — good citizens, all — were encroaching on his independence. My photo of him amid his rubble seemed like Grant Wood's *American Gothic,* with a mastiff in place of the wife.

When Roy read the piece he stopped the presses, added my byline, and came across to the café where I was having lunch. "If you're ever applying for a newspaper job somewhere, make sure you show them that story with that picture. That will get you hired anywhere."

Of course, I was flattered. But also disappointed. I'd missed my chance to hear: "Stop the presses!"

Then there was the day when I covered the airport arrival of Queen Elizabeth and Prince Phillip in 1959. I forget whether I'd arrived too late, or had trouble parking, or had otherwise screwed up, but I found myself smack next to the limo as it slowly drew away from the curb. As I stumbled along beside it, getting whacked both by my flapping raincoat and by the leather camera case, desperately trying to frame a shot, I saw the prince laughing at me.

So I didn't get my snap of the royal couple. But I got a laugh out of Prince Phillip. That's good enough.

In that climate people accused me of all sorts of viciousness. Even recently an Israeli attorney charged that, in late February 1948, I grabbed three Haganah members at Mandelbaum Gate, next to Jerusalem's Old City, and turned them over to an Arab mob to murder. But I'd left Palestine in October 1947. For good, needless to say.

That's the kind of lies I've always been up against. Fortunately, they did not affect my court martial.

Following my acquittal, I was hustled out under heavy guard for a night in Gaza and then shipped out to Liverpool, on the troopship *Orduna*. For security reasons I was let off the ship half an hour before anyone else.

As I stepped out, to my surprise I was cheered by hundreds of troops. The trial had made me a hero.[15]

Sadly, at the time Liverpool was in the grips of a serious outburst of anti-Semitism. There'd been anti-Jewish riots in August, an arson attack on

a Jewish furniture store, the smash-
ing of a clothier's. I suppose there's
always been some anti-Jewish feeling among Britons, which the Jewish
bombings in Palestine had enflamed.

I'm afraid that may still hold true.
It's not a prejudice, mind. We're just
aware that the Jews are so different
from us.

After my first summer Roy kept me on as a stringer.
He paid me 25 cents a column-inch to follow up on
North Hill stories. My cheerleader series led to high
school sports. For two bits an inch, I really shovelled
it: "Fullback 'Grindin' Graydon' Morrison, 16-year-old
son of Mr. and Mrs. Gordon Morrison of 115 Cambrian
Drive NW, picked up three yards behind a brutal block
by 17-year-old guard..."

An inveterate couch potato, I was thrilled to attach
myself, however vicariously, to the Crescent Heights
star athletes. Dave Horodetsky, Barry Luft, Kit Lefroy:
these remain names to conjure with. Of course Central High had its own stars, who even won the Alberta
football championship: Tony Reed, Henry Mandin,
Ross Christensen, Sheldon Chumir, Currie Harbour,
John Harrop, Jerry Shaw. But at Central I was just a

fan. With the Crescent Heights stars my relationship was professional.

Nor was I limited to the athletes: "Another citizenship award for Maureen Mulholland, 16-year-old daughter of Mrs. Irene Mulholland of 2124 Victoria Crescent NW..."

I made a pile off of Fran Van Sant, who was not only a star athlete but a citizenship whiz, an honour student, and what-have-you. She became a teacher. Years later I was delighted to meet her and learn she'd spent her career back at Crescent Heights. She loved that school, and for once the ardour was reciprocated.

Tuesday nights I would drop my copy off at Roy's house, along with clippings of my previous week's work and an accompanying invoice. At about nine he'd just be back home, sitting down to dinner. His wife, Ruth, was a gracious, beautiful woman.

I had never seen asparagus before.

My dad would joke about my weekly invoice. "My son had sixty-five inches last week. Not bad for a *boychik*."

When I returned to work full time at the paper in the summer of 1959, I suggested that I continue to be paid at the space rate. At 25 cents an inch I would have made a fortune. But no, Roy put me back on the apprentice scale. This meant a raise to $24.15 a week, net.

When I received my Legion of Merit medal from the Americans, my parents were proud witnesses.

But we were all rather on edge because of threats we had been receiving in the mail. We'd get letters with one word: *Nakama*. That's Hebrew for "revenge."

Come to think of it, isn't *nashama* their word for "soul"? Odd equation. One of those telling accidents of language, I suppose.

Once Roy warned me off a career in journalism: "You know, Morris, there's no money in it. Even this operation doesn't make much. My money comes from my books. You should think about that. You're a good writer."

He recommended travel writing. "You could see the world, and there's good money in it."

Roy was currently on a campaign to change the system used to elect city aldermen. The City of Calgary, he argued, was getting too large to handle neighbourhood issues. A ward system would elect aldermen by district and hold them accountable if they failed to solve local problems. Made sense to me.

On May 3rd, 1948, my younger brother, Rex, was at my parents' home in Codsall, Wolverhampton. He was taking a nap. I was visiting friends in Scotland; my parents were out walking. The postwoman, a wonderful gal, Eileen Hayes, passed them on the road and said she had only a parcel for them. "One of the boys will take it," my mum answered.

Rex woke up to find a package addressed to R. Farran, so he opened it. The bomb blew out the windows and ripped out his stomach. He was twenty-five. My other brother, Keith, who was just eighteen, called the ambulance right off, but Rex died two hours later.

Rex. Do you know what his last words were? "Am I brave enough for a Farran?" Then: "No revenge." Dear Rex. We used to call him "Pud."

His funeral service was held under a very tight police guard.

No one was ever charged with Rex's murder. But I am absolutely certain his killer was an East London Jew from the Zionist Hebrew Legion, Monty Harris. He was sentenced to seven years for making and mailing bombs. That's a far cry from the hanging the Jewish press still demanded for me. And I had been properly acquitted.

Harris was probably also involved in sending a similar explosive, gelignite, wrapped in a role of periodicals mailed to the home of General Sir Evelyn Barker, the former General Officer Commanding in Palestine. He lived in Cobham, Surrey. He had been on the Stern Gang's hit list since '46.

The package was delivered to Lady Barker in her bedroom. Fortunately, before she opened it completely she noticed the package's weight and then spotted a telltale wire and a bit of black insulating tape. She cast it aside and so narrowly averted death.[16]

That was the Stern Gang for you.

One morning Roy breezed in with a scoop for me.

"You like movies. A downtown cinema manager has been charged with raping an employee. Over several months. She says she kept working there because she couldn't get another job. The manager kept raping her. He is also said to have beaten up a truck driver who stole his girl."

"I didn't see that in the papers."

"They won't cover it. They get too much money from the cinema ads. That's where we come in. Cinemas don't advertise here. But there's something else. The accused is defended by his brother, and they're from a very prominent Jewish family."

I recognized the name.

"Do you mind taking this on?"

"No, it's fine."

"Then go to the trial, perhaps interview the plaintiffs for a sidebar. Give me your copy early because we'll want to run every word past our lawyer."

I went, I watched, I interviewed the girl and the burly, bruised trucker. He was much bigger than the cinema manager. Embarrassed, he told me that his size was no help against the manager's brass knuckles and meaner spirit.

After the first two stories ran, I got a phone call at work. It was the defence lawyer.

"I've wanted to meet you for some time, Maurice.

May I call you Maurice?"

"Sure."

"I understand you were president of AZA. My mother speaks highly of your mother, from the Reader's Circle. She tells me you're planning on law school. When you're looking to intern, I would certainly like to discuss your plans with you. But for now I just have one question. Why is an intelligent Jewish boy working for a known anti-Semite like Roy Farran?"

"I have not seen any sign of anti-Semitism in Mr. Farran. He's an exceptional public servant."

"That's very touching. But why do you side with a man who killed a young Jewish boy? And why should a Jew be the only reporter publishing vicious lies about my brother? I assure you he will be found completely innocent. Then you will have to live with having libelled your own people."

"Well, our lawyers assure us nothing I've written is libellous. I hope your guy is found innocent, if he *is* innocent. Democracy depends on public trials. I'm rather proud our paper is the only one covering his trial. Guilty or innocent, the verdict will be out in the open. I hope to cover this trial to the end, but, of course, it's Mr. Farran's decision."

"Young man, you are not as smart as you think. If you continue on this path, you will find yourself very, very alone. I will keep my eye on you."

"Good. Thanks for calling."

A week and a news story later Roy told me: "You don't have to go to court tomorrow. There's been a cash settlement."

"Damn. I hoped we'd stay on it till the end."

"But we did. Don't you see? We won. Without your stories the family would never have settled. They have the money to face the victims down. But the publicity scared them off. Well done."

At the time, it was easy for me to prefer the crusading editor over the high-class, sleazy lawyer.

After leaving the army I was at loose ends. I worked in a quarry in Scotland. Then for Keir & Cawder of Glasgow on the Loch Sloy hydroelectric scheme. In 1948 they sent me to Southern Rhodesia as managing director.

It was in Salisbury that I met Ruth Harvie Ardern. She was beautiful, smart, sociable, and she shared my passion for horses. Ruth's father was William Ardern. He ranched in Canada, outside Calgary. The original OH Ranch, founded back in 1883.

Now, I'd had my share of beautiful

women, I must say. Back then I cut a figure. I was only five-foot-eight, but the ladies loved the sparkle in my blue eyes. They didn't have Paul Newman yet, you see.

I was essentially shy, but women seemed to arouse my love of life. I tell you, when I worked in the Greek underground, I had to fight them off. I remember one, Elpice . . .

I lived with an Italian partisan, Norice, all through Operation Tombola. You could drown in her grey eyes and long black hair. She was one of our *staffeta,* girls who cooked and cleaned for us. They'd bicycle down to flirt with the Jerrys and then tell us all they saw. I may have mentioned her work in my Tombola memoir. I hope I was gentleman enough not to divulge our affair.

But Ruth was my love for life. We very soon agreed to marry.

I suppose Roy Farran became a second father to me. His encouragement, his guidance. I was growing up under him. But I began to disagree with some of his opinions. Especially when he took potshots at the university.

One of the original appointments in English at UAC, Dr. Birgitta Steene, was in New Orleans reporting on an integrated school for a Swedish paper. At a demonstration down there some racist women pelted her with eggs. The *Herald* picked up the story from the Canadian Press. Roy wrote a critical editorial: "The university pays its professors to stay here and teach, not to go off to meddle in other people's business."

I was sorry he didn't see the higher value. When I took Professor Steene's North American Lit course I wanted to apologize. But I didn't.

Roy also attacked Professor Ian Adam for his sabbatical research: "George Eliot? Why should the Calgary taxpayer pay a professor to go reread George Eliot for a year?" As it happened, Professor Adam soon became one of my mentors.[17]

My theory was that the press resented universities because they were rivals in shaping the community's thought. Perhaps ironically, in his post-politics years Roy would occasionally lecture on political science at the University of Alberta.

Roy also had me expose the Communist background of a classical pianist from Edmonton. I felt queasy about this — it smacked of McCarthyism. But I did it.

This assignment had an unfortunate consequence.

At a City Council meeting, I was chatting with a young reporter from *The Albertan* — Calgary's morning daily, long since defunct. He was one of Roy's drinking buddies. He asked whether I had anything good for the next day's paper. Foolishly, I bragged about my exposé of the pianist. The next morning *The Albertan* carried a rebuttal, with a quote from the pianist. They scooped our scoop.

Roy was furious. It turned out that, after the meeting ended, his young reporter friend had come over to the *North Hill News* and cajoled an advance copy of the paper out of one of the night staff, on the pretext that he was on his way to the airport to leave the country. Then he'd done his story, undercutting ours entirely. Over drinks that night, he teased Roy about how he'd duped the paper's naïve staff.

For Frank, the pressman who had innocently provided the paper, Roy worked out a punishment with the shop union rep. For me he had another:

"If we were a big daily, I'd assign you to the morgue for a month. All you'd do would be obituaries. But we're not, so we've had to figure out something else. I've talked with Bill. You will have to work nights all of next week. I've come up with five evening meetings for you to cover. We may not have room for all the stories, but you'll have to write them anyway. That should teach you to keep your mouth shut."

I didn't tell my parents or my three best pals — Alan Arthur, Irving Rootman, and Elliot Gelfand — that I was being punished. It was just an especially busy week, with several important meetings that Mr. Farran couldn't cover himself. I managed to impress them with what was really my shame.

I was torn. Part of me couldn't help worrying that Roy would rather have that bright, aggressive *Albertan* reporter working for him than me. If nothing else, they would drink together. At the same time, I was furious that I was being punished for the impulse to boast about our paper, for taking pride in a good story. It was a story I was ashamed of doing, but still . . .

I considered quitting. At the very least, I told myself, I would serve out the punishment — take it like a man — and then confront Mr. Farran with the unfairness of his judgement.

In the event, I did neither. In fact, I enjoyed the work so much that the punishment didn't feel like a punishment.

In October 1949, I won the Conservative nomination for my home riding of Dudley-Stourbridge, despite charges that I was an anti-Semitic fascist. That's politics for you. But in the end

I lost to Labour. Their Colonel George Wigg was the undersecretary of war and a known Zionist and leftist.

For a while I raised cattle in Worcestershire. I offered my guerrilla expertise for use in the Korean War but was rejected. An old chum's invitation to join his new squadron in Malaya was vetoed.

Ruth and I married, and in August 1950 we moved to Calgary. At the age of twenty-nine, I was retiring to the colonies.

I initially planned to run a dairy farm in Springbank but turned instead to writing a novel, *Jungle Chase*. It was based on my experiences in East Africa. My memoir, *Winged Dagger*, written back in 1948, had sold so well that I'd been able to pay off my legal debts and have enough left over for a comfortable life.

In 1952 I joined the *Calgary Herald* as a reporter. I learned the lay of the land. Two years later I founded the *North Hill News*. Though it was a small community paper, it provided me with a good platform. It also left me time to write other books. There was my history of the Calgary Highlanders. Then, in 1960, I wrote another memoir, *Operation Tombola*. Also a few novels. In fact, a couple of my novels I serialized in our paper. Like Dickens.

As my second summer drew to an end, Roy made a tempting offer.

"You know, Morris, you don't have to go back to university. Let's face it, no matter what happens, you are going to be a journalist. It's in your blood. Instead of going back to school, why don't you take over from me here? I'd like to pull back from this work, perhaps try my hand at politics. The new ward system should give me a shot at City Council. If you take over for me as editor, I'll pay you $400 a month. That's good money."

I thanked Roy and said I would talk it over with my parents.

In the end, I took my dad's advice: "If you're worth $400 a month now, Moishele, what will you get with a degree? Maybe $500?"

Roy was not surprised by my decision. A few months later I dropped in to ask about a summer job for 1960.

"Of course, we'd be delighted to have you back. There'll be some change, though. I'm running for Council, so I'm bringing in a new editor, Graham Smith. He's another Englishman. He worked for the *Guardian* but trained on tabloids. You'll get on fine."

"It'll be nice to meet him. But there's one problem. Now I'm at university, I'll need more money."

"Yes. Well, perhaps we could go — $45 a week?"

"Great. Thanks."

"You know, for all the education we're giving you here, you should be paying us."

World War II won me my decorations and my reputation in guerrilla warfare.

The war broke out when I was an eighteen-year-old cadet in the 3rd Carabiniers (Prince of Wales's Dragoon Guards). I was a troop leader at nineteen.

My first military success came in 1940, in Sir Archibald Wavell's Operation Compass. My light tanks squadron, the 3rd King's Own Hussars, helped rout the Italian army at Sidi Barrani, in North Africa. That was a three-month fight. Though Marshal Graziani had far superior numbers, we took twenty-five thousand prisoners and gave Britain her first land victory of the war. Remarkable. We cleared Cyrenaica of the enemy — temporarily. Until General Rommel and his Africa Korps undid our work.[18]

I liked Graham. He was a remarkable man in his own right. He had joined the RAF, flew a Mosquito, and was invited into the Pathfinder No. 18 Squadron. Later on, Grant MacEwan — writer, mayor of Calgary, and then lieutenant-governor — would call him the best journalist in Alberta.

Graham was less intimidating than Roy and more effusive, with his bushy eyebrows and a soup-strainer moustache. He even said "By Jove!"

He also had a knack for debunking common assumptions.

"Everyone says Calgary is a coffee-drinking town, but you know, Morris, statistics show that more Calgarians drink tea than coffee." (Graham favoured tea.)

"The dailies pay far too much attention to the professional hockey and football teams. They've become the teams' unpaid flacks. The public would far rather read about school sports, amateur games. And many of us would appreciate reports on real football, what you here call soccer." Graham very efficiently taught me the rules so I could pick up a few dollars doing PR for the Alberta Soccer League.

He also put me onto *I'm All Right Jack*, the movie and the novel, as an insightful representation of union excesses in Britain and thus a warning for us.

My summer with Graham was a series of delightful and illuminating chats. I would thereafter always enjoy visiting him on my trips home to Calgary.[19] Nonetheless, I was disappointed that Roy was rarely around that last summer.

In all our time together, Roy and I had only two conversations that related to his private life. The first was when he was deciding whether to send his children through the Catholic or the public school system. I assured him that my early education at the Jewish school — the I.L. Peretz School — had, if anything, proved an advantage when I went to public school.

The other was during my second summer, after I'd heard all those Roy Farran stories. One morning Roy dropped the day's mail on my desk, as usual. But when I began to rip open a package, he stopped me.

"Hold on there. You could blow your head off that way. If that held a bomb instead of a book, we'd both be dead. Here's how you do it." He came over to demonstrate. "Keep the pressure on the package until you can see what's inside. So. Press down, lift the flap, look in. There, it's a book, fine, now you can open it. Safely."

There was a gleam in Roy's eye as he taught this Jewish boy how to avoid being blown up by a piece of mail.

I've read his eyes described as killer cold. With me he was rarely anything but soft and genial. But sometimes when I glimpsed him coming out of a closed-door meeting, I was struck by the odd hardness in his gaze.

When we were brought in to reinforce the New Zealand infantry at the battle of Galatas, in Crete, I was wounded in my right arm and both legs. The Germans overran the hospital and flew me to a POW camp near Athens, where I recuperated for a while. This was 1941. One day, when a guard dozed off, I put on these civvy shorts I'd hidden away and, wearing nothing else, crawled under the perimeter fence and escaped.

The Greek underground put me in touch with another batch of escapees.

I've never forgotten the kindness of Elisabeth Paschakis and her family. They helped to save us. The Nazis eventually took her and her children, but she escaped.

With provisions for only four days, I and fourteen other British POWs left in a fishing boat from Piraeus. We were headed for Egypt, but a storm drove us off course. We ran out of diesel fuel, food, water. But after ten days mercy smiled and we were picked up, exhausted, by a Royal Navy destroyer forty miles north of Alexandria. I was awarded my first Military Cross for my gallantry in Crete and a second for leading those escaped POWs to safety.

I based my novel *The Day After Tomorrow* on my experiences in Greece. It's a memoir turned somewhat into fiction. Tricky business, that, but readers took it well.[20]

In the spring of 1960, late in my first year at UAC, the Students' Union appointed me editor of the university paper for the upcoming school year. Until then, the *Cal-Var* had been a mimeographed monthly sheet consisting mainly of sports scores. I proposed instead to produce a weekly of at least eight pages, professionally printed, to be financed by ad sales.

I suggested naming it *The Gauntlet*. But, ever democratic, the Union insisted we hold a contest to choose the paper's new name. They offered a $15 prize. There were fourteen entries, all from me. They chose *The Gauntlet*. As editor-elect, however, I could not claim the prize.

The image of running a gauntlet was my version of Roy's motto, "Without Fear or Favour." Our logo was an armoured knight. *Furor arma ministrat:* "Rage is its own weapon." It is, you know, as terrorists (and students) have long known.

All that summer I stashed ideas and wrote pieces for *The Gauntlet* even as I worked for Roy. In my spare time I wrote the humour issue I planned to put out at the end of exam week the first semester. I titled it *Maieutic*, to place our sophomoric wit in the tradition of Socratic subversion. For the second-term exam week I planned a literary issue. I figured these exam-week issues would serve a double purpose. Coming off the exams, the students would get a bonus publication. But it would also appear that I and my staff had time to produce these extra issues while we were studying for and writing our exams.

My *Gauntlet* year, 1960–61, was a year of new beginnings for UAC. Malcolm G. Taylor, a professor of political science from the University of Victoria, was our new principal, supplanting Andrew Doucette.

That fall the university moved from its wing at the Tech to a new campus on the city's northwest frontier. The first building to open was MacMahon Stadium, rushed to completion in time for the Stampeders' season. The two academic buildings had to take a back seat and were not quite finished when the fall term began. Our former mayor, Don Mackay, had secured for the church he attended a development site between the main campus and the stadium.

Other than MacMahon, the two academic buildings — flat, low-lying structures now known as Administration and Science A — were the only marks on the empty prairie. There was not a tree or a blade of grass. The dust blew so badly that one had to wash after walking between the buildings.

Before the term began, the new Principal Taylor invited me to lunch. He wanted to discuss my plans for the school paper. He hadn't moved his family from Victoria yet, so he was staying at the Palliser, at the time Calgary's best. Too nervous to meet him alone, I asked if I could bring along my more sophisticated assistant editor, Alan Arthur. Alan had been one of my best friends since Grade Nine.

"By all means," Principal Taylor said. "All the better."

At lunch I ordered the Salisbury steak, which unnervingly turned out to be hamburger. My editorship would be a wide-ranging learning experience.

"What kind of paper are you planning?" Principal Taylor asked.

"Well, I'm not going to be an Angry Young Man or anything like that."

"Why not?"

I suspect that, if Principal Taylor later remembered encouraging me to social criticism, he may have come to regret it. Over the course of the year he would find occasions to be deeply disappointed in the paper — and in me.

The Gauntlet went well at first. We put out a paper of at least sixteen pages each week, while I carried a full course load in second-year English. As I recall, I was given a $100 honorarium. Thanks to Barry Law, an accomplished layout man from Saskatchewan, the paper looked smart. With Morris Bleviss as business manager and Morris Dancyger as advertising director, it managed to pay its own way. My old friends Susan Aisenman and Alan Arthur were my very capable news and assistant editors, respectively.

To keep the dust down, the university deposited a layer of manure. The olfactory effect was every bit as bad as the dust. We printed one issue in brown ink that was supposed to smell like manure, but the aroma quickly faded. More successful was our Blood Drive edition: "This week's bloody issue of *The UAC Gauntlet*," in red ink, with such nagging fillers as "Be a sport, give a quart" and — in homage to *Mad Magazine*'s running gag — "Axolotl gave a bottle."

My editorial against starting American-style fraternities on our small campus prompted a positive report in *The Albertan*. And, before a roomful of students, an education prof quoted my editorial exhorting instructors to distribute written lecture notes so that class time could be devoted to discussion. True, Principal Taylor was not happy when we reported that he had gotten a speeding ticket on the highway. He'd been distracted by his daughter Deanna's impersonation of Shelley Berman, he explained. He said he felt I was persecuting him with a minor, embarrassing story, but I thought a paper had to report candidly on the powerful.

Those were such different times. A group of Russian students spent a day on campus as part of their national tour. That was a big deal. The Red Menace in our midst! Something had to be done. Above the masthead we ran in Cyrillic the Russian word for "Welcome." *Strasvitznieh*, I think it was. We felt brave.

In short, *The Gauntlet* was proceeding smoothly. Perhaps too smoothly.

At the start of 1942, I was assigned to the 7th Armoured Division. I was aide-de-camp to Major General Jock Campbell, the division commander. On February 26th, I was driving him back from a tour of the Gazala front when I lost control on a patch of newly laid clay. The car overturned. I was thrown clear, but General Campbell was killed instantly.

I have to say, as I lay in the desert alone, the other riders still unconscious, I considered suicide. I felt such a failure. I had ended a good man's life. Perhaps because I have always felt my Catholicism profoundly, this experience left me deeply shaken.

I was grateful when the new commander kept me on his staff.[21]

When I ran a rearguard unit in the 8th Army's retreat from Gazala, I picked up some bad arm wounds in a bombing and was sent home.

Back in England, I just couldn't fit in. I begged the medical board to declare me fit and then the army to send me back to the 8th. I was still cooling my heels when an old pal, Sandy Scratchley, got me into the Special Air Service.

I was back in North Africa in early 1943 for parachute training. In May I was second-in-command of a squadron. Although I had malaria, I insisted on leading a raid on a lighthouse at Cape Passero, on the southeast coast of Sicily, which housed some machine-gun units.

In September I commanded reconnaissance and sabotage operations in southern Italy. On October 27th my SAS unit dropped north of the River Tronto, behind the German lines. For five days we scuttled about, blowing up the railway line, cutting telephone communications, destroying enemy transport.

In late October, at a Sunday evening meeting at Diane Bailey's house, we kicked around ideas for the next issue of the paper. Diane was a member of our high school discussion group that now formed the core of *The Gauntlet*'s unofficial editorial board.

"We have that philosophical argument for atheism."

"That'll stir up some shit. Let's run it."

"Is it good?"

"Persuasive. Just what this Bible Belt school needs."

"But that's a back-page article. We still need an editorial."

"How about the Stampede? It's so silly to pretend we're still cowboys. It's 1960, for God's sake. And holding a livestock show, when there's a scrapies epidemic?"

"Maybe save that till closer to the Stampede. Good ideas though."

"Isn't next Friday Remembrance Day?"

"Yes! Perfect! There's too much war, and Remembrance Day encourages wars. That's it." I started to write: "Don't buy a poppy on Remembrance Day. The institution celebrates war not peace. It encourages old generals to turn young men into cannon fodder. We sneer at conscientious objectors while we honour warmongers and faceless blobs. Such rituals encourage more wars."

"Well, that's a start," I said. "I'll work on it."

As I remember, Diane's father, Frank Bailey — the popular Calgary bandleader — was out on a gig, but Mrs. Bailey was there. "Won't that get you into trouble?" she asked.

"All the better," said the always spirited Alan Arthur. "We'll take copies to the Jubilee Auditorium to pass out at the Canadian Legion rally. We can say: 'Let's we forget.'"

In mid-August 1944 I took sixty men and twenty Jeeps two hundred miles behind enemy lines to Châtillon-sur-Seine, north of Dijon. This was known as Operation Wallace. Since escaping from the Germans in Greece, I was operating under the name Patrick Mc-Ginty. I took the name from a song about an Irish goat that swallowed a stick of dynamite.

We killed some five hundred Germans, destroyed twenty-three staff cars, six motorcycles, thirty-six trucks and troop carriers — plus a goods train and a supply dump holding a hundred thousand gallons of petrol. Our casualties were light: only seven killed, two wounded, one MIA, and two captured. At Beaulieu the Germans panicked, blew up their wireless station, and evacuated. Wallace was one of the SAS's most successful post-D-Day operations.

The Jerrys had already lost Normandy. Our push east from Rennes through the German-occupied Darney forest to Belfort, in effect attacking the Germans from within, was a tremendous help to the French Resistance.

I must say, I was extremely impressed by the courage and the spirit of the French Resistance. Their hunger to reclaim their freedom, their nation, was palpable. One magnificent woman, her smile laughed away the bullets.

I — or rather Patrick McGinty — was given a DSO for that, but I was also scolded for taking my squadron on an illicit leave in Paris en route back. *C'est la guerre.* Remember, I was twenty-three at the time, still a tad frisky.

When the November 11th *Gauntlet* appeared, nobody even noticed the atheism essay. The talk on campus —

and in editorials in the Calgary dailies and on radio talk shows — was about my Poppy Day editorial. It was the university's first huge scandal.

The editorial's position could have been argued coolly, logically, even persuasively. But I was young and heated. So, like many a young crusader, I made a visceral argument instead. I was angry, not clear. I admit the editorial was insensitive, an exercise in bellicose pacifism.

But I was not prepared for the backlash. To this day, it astonishes me. At home we had to take the phone off the hook because of calls from parents of Calgary soldiers — my "warmongers and faceless blobs."

A few said that although they hated what I'd written, they respected me and would defend my right to say it. That comforted my folks. But one caller from the Canadian Legion warned them of plans to plant a bomb in my car. For my '51 Austin — that I had to put in reverse to get up the 14th Street North hill — this seemed like not an entirely bad idea. All the same, I put Scotch tape on the hood so that I could tell whether it had been opened.

What surprised me most was that complete strangers kept referring to "my people." The fact that I was Jewish had nowhere appeared in print, but somehow word got around the city.

My favourite call came from the lawyer who had pressured me over covering his cinema manager brother's rape trial:

"Maurice, you don't know me, but I am calling on behalf of the B'nai Brith. I've been appointed chair of a small committee assigned to take you on a tour of the graves of Calgary's Jewish veterans. We'd like to give you a lesson in intellectual honesty."

"It's good to chat with you again, but I'll pass, thanks. Good night."

Frankly, that bravado was false. I did not feel good. I was miserable at the thought that I had caused families such pain. Also, I was afraid that by writing that editorial I had forever ruined my professional career. Whatever my eventual profession. But my parents stood behind me, sympathetic and encouraging, and so did my friends.

When Principal Taylor summoned me, my expectations hovered between expulsion and decapitation. As I stood in his outer office, sweat trickling icily down my armpits, a string of his senior faculty filed out. Professor Schonfield, from whom I was taking a psychology class, averted his gaze, but the head of the English Department, Earl Guy, ventured a quick wink as he passed. That gave me the nerve to go in.

Principal Taylor assured me that he had rejected all the suggestions that I be expelled. Of decapitation he discreetly made no mention. I was to be suspended from the editorship of *The Gauntlet* for three weeks, during which time Alan would run the paper. In addition, I was to research and write three essays for Principal Taylor: one on the origin of Poppy Day, one on the Nazis' treatment of the Jews, and one on the work of the Canadian Legion. Thanks to my *North Hill News* experience I finished them all in a week, but I shelved them until the due date.

Researching the essays proved instructive. I learned that Poppy Day was a response to the rather less noble World War I, not the World War II purportedly waged to save "my people" from extermination. My respect for the work of the Canadian Legion led me to question why it should even be necessary, why respect for our veterans and for our fallen did not translate into sufficient government support — social, medical, and financial — for our heroes and their families. My essay on World War II focused on instances of sadistic treatment of the Jews and the outside world's documented indifference.

"That's not an essay I'd accept in my political science class," Principal Taylor remarked of the latter.

"I didn't write it for your political science class."

"That's true."

I returned to *The Gauntlet* properly chastened.

It took me a month to muster the courage to face

Mr. Farran. He'd sent me a letter explaining how some wars were necessary and why we need soldiers whose sacrifice preserves our values. He later told me that he meant it as a personal note, but we had run it among the other letters in the next issue.

When I finally dropped by the *North Hills News* office, I apologized for the embarrassment I'd caused him.

"That's fine, Morris. It's behind us now. Good job you screwed up so early in your career. You'll bounce back, what?"

We would drop behind enemy lines, in Italy, in France, then attack airfields, roads, fuel supplies. We gave the partisans some crash training. We'd wreak what havoc we could to soften Jerry up for our front line's attack. I'm sure we caused psychological damage well beyond the Germans' casualty roll. Make the enemy feel insecure and you're halfway home. The terrorists knew that too.

That was the life. No military bureaucracy. No police restraints. Catch as catch can — in the field. We learned

pinpoint firing, shooting to kill, unarmed mortal combat. That was hon-
est warfare. Damned sight better than
watching terrorists coddled and set
free.

Still, sometimes I just *had* to dis-
obey orders. Without formal sanction I
snuck off to Greece to thank the people
in Athens who'd helped me escape in
'41. The sad thing was to see — what
with the Germans now departed — a
vicious civil war going on between the
government and the commies.

From Greece I was summoned to
Operation Tombola, which was intended to invigorate the Italian partisans
in Reggio. That we certainly did.[22]

We and a 70mm howitzer were
dropped into the mountains between
Spezia and Genoa. My battalion of
Allied troops — a motley crew of SAS
commandos, Italian partisans, and
escaped Russian prisoners — attacked
the Germans' HQ, based at two villas
near Albinea and protected by Span-
dau machine-gun posts sited at stra-
tegic points.

Now, I had made a serious error of judgement. I'd ordered an attack on the Brenner Pass despite horrendous weather. It was a disaster, and we lost some valuable, experienced leaders. I felt so guilty about their deaths that I could not accept my orders to control the Albinea attack from the safety of Florence. Instead, I finagled a lift on an American aircraft. I contrived to fall out of the plane over a mountain east of La Spezia. I was wearing my parachute. There I met up with my men. After the Brenner fiasco I simply had to lead that operation myself. No matter what I'd been told.

Then I ordered the attack on Albinea, despite orders to delay. The remote command couldn't possibly know what we on the spot knew. Besides, I was afraid my men would lose their boil, their edge. Unfortunately, back in Florence I learned that knocking out the HQ was supposed to coincide with a main force offensive. I had screwed that up, too.

But our success saved my neck. We

killed about six hundred Germans and took four hundred prisoners. The British intended to court-martial me, but when the Americans awarded me their Legion of Merit, my countrymen underwent a change of heart. Fifty years later, the people of Albinea immortalized my "Allied battalion" by naming their town square "Piazza del Battaglione Alleato."

I was called a loose cannon. A daredevil. But who dares, wins.

I had ordered up a piper, Kirkpatrick, to raise our partisans' spirits as much as our own. It worked, especially when we attacked Albinea to the tune of his "Highland Laddie."

Loose cannon, what?

———

I still wonder why I wrote that editorial. Who knows why anyone wrecks himself.

My motives may have been good. Like generating a debate on an unquestioned assumption. Or involving this new university — which, so young and so small, seemed more like a glorified high school — in some serious argument. As for my vitriolic language, I unwittingly anticipated the anti-war anger that Vietnam soon provoked. But all that is hindsight, which may not be the most accurate perspective.

And yet I still wonder whether I was overcome by some self-destructive urge. Did I need to do something to spoil the paper's early success? Did I feel compelled to take a dangerous plunge, minus a safety net?

Or was that anti-war rant my revolt against my second father figure? Perhaps I needed to adopt a belligerent pacifism to break free from that war hero. Like I had to upset my parents by dating shiksas.

I made up for the scandal I'd created with a spectacular Christmas edition. The front and back pages were quietly reverent. But the paper's highlight was a thirteen-colour half-page picture of an "olde print shoppe" inscribed with a Christmas greeting from our printer, Bill Randall, who wanted to show off his new colour offset press.

Principal Taylor sent copies up to the University Senate in Edmonton.

But the prodigal editor had not long to remain. On Valentine's Day, we published the campus's first literary magazine, *Callidus*. An Irish graduate student in physics, John Emberson, contributed a short story titled *Perdu*. In the recently legalized manner of D.H. Lawrence, it contained the line: "He came into her, and it was good."

Provost Gibb read the line, panicked, and confiscated all the copies from the stands. When he stormed into the *Gauntlet* office to seize the rest, he found some staffers conducting a séance. That did not mollify him.

One of the students reported the seizure to a radio station. Again the dailies and the talk shows fueled the scandal. This time they supported me, especially the radio jocks:

"Aw, come on now, you eggheads in the ivory tower out there on the lunatic fringe of our city. University students are supposed to be adults. Why shouldn't they read about sex? Some of them may even be doing it! Maybe even the married ones. Sometimes I worry about our Alberta."

But the Students' Union had had enough. They had appointed me to edit the newspaper, not a literary magazine, they declared, so they fired me. Only Joyce Kunelius, the student rep from Education, voted to keep me.

* * *

Come to think of it, I'd made good money covering Joyce's high school successes for the *North Hill News*. "Joyce Kunelius, 15-year-old daughter of Mr. and Mrs. Leo Kunelius of . . ." Damn, can't remember the address. In Briar Hill, kitty-corner from Reuben Hashman's pharmacy. In her first year, she was the Engineers' candidate for campus Queen. Brother Eric, sisters Karen and Ingrid, Joyce was the oldest.

The memory. It gleams; it fades.

I contrived to get back to Athens for the liberation of Greece. Then to London for V-E Day.

What a night. We climbed onto the Palace Theatre roof for the best view of the drama.

I woke up late the next morning sprawled under a tree in Hyde Park. I'm not sure I still had my trousers on.

Immediately — I missed the war. The campaigns, the men, the danger. I certainly celebrated the peace, but immediately — emptiness.

You see, I had always expected to be killed in battle. I woke up stranded, spared by some odd trick of fate.[23]

I rejoined the 3rd King's Own Hussars to drive the French out of Syria.

Roy cheered me up when I visited.

"Well, Morris. Congratulations. You managed to

leave in a burst of glory. Firing you was absurd. I'm as perturbed as anyone by all this new vulgarity, but that story was quite innocuous. They should have applauded your literary initiative, not fired you."

"Thanks, sir. I appreciate that."

"You know, you can certainly be proud of your *Gauntlet*. It looked professional. It stirred up debate. I'm only sorry you didn't bring us the printing instead of Northwest."

"I didn't want any appearance of conflict of interest. You can bid on it for next year. It comes out Fridays so you can do it after your paper's out."

"Will you come back here in the spring?"

"I didn't think you'd want me, after all that."

"Nonsense. You're a better newspaperman than ever. Tempered by experience. Like steel."

"Thanks. I appreciate that."

"What did we pay you last year?"

"I think it was $45 a week."

"We should be able to go to $50. What do you say?"

"Well, I appreciate your offer, but I'd better wait. I really need to make more money to start saving for grad school."

"The job is open. If you don't find anything else, start here and you can leave if something better turns up. No hard feelings."

In the summer of 1961 I did start out at the paper

but soon quit. I was the second person hired by Bob Elston when he introduced pizza to Calgary in the form of Ye Olde Pizza Joint. But I kept in touch with the paper. Indeed, on a hot day I arranged for the *North Hill News* to run a picture of Bob baking a pizza on the sidewalk in front of his shop.

Perhaps because of my colourful background, people assume I was born in India. I may have suggested that myself. In fact, I was born in England, very near Dudley. Immediately after, the RAF posted my father, a warrant officer, to India. I grew up at the cavalry station of Risalpur, on the North-West Frontier. That's where I got my lifelong love for horses. That's also where I picked up Hindustani.

One of my earliest memories, I was six, my father and I were caught in a nationalist riot. A mob had already killed two Europeans, and now they surrounded our car. Father put his service revolver to our driver's head and forced him to drive straight through the mob to safety.

That's when I discovered the thrill of danger. And how to persuade a reluctant cabbie. That mob taught me to uphold the British Empire. I owe to my father my soldier's courage, my Catholic faith — and the Irishman's suspicion of authority. Any authority.[24]

The UAC students were forgiving. After my *Gauntlet* firing, I was elected campus chair of the National Federation of Canadian University Students.

Indeed, I won the NFCUS national essay prize for my "Notes on the Firing of University Student Editors." The paper went beyond my own experience — for the same year I was fired, the University of Saskatchewan Students' Union canned their *Sheaf* editor, Danny Bereskin. Some twelve years earlier, Danny had been the older boy who used to resent his mother's orders to play with me when my mother visited her, around the corner from my grandmother's home on Angus Crescent in Regina.

The following year I was elected president of the Students' Union. My term passed without any major public scandal or any serious dispute (or noteworthy success) with Principal Taylor.

As student body president, I drove out to the airport

to meet our first two African students, who had won scholarships from (I believe) the Calgary Rotary Club. I drove the men to the basement apartment the university had found for them to share, within walking distance of the open prairie campus. By the time I returned to the Union office, they'd phoned. Could I come talk to the landlord? The men had expected to share a single bedroom, fine, but not a single bed. We quickly straightened that one out. I enjoyed the job.

The two Africans were charming — shy but friendly fellows. Their years here must have been difficult indeed, what with their families left behind, but they threw themselves in. Moses Chirambo was a long-distance runner who became Malawi's first ophthalmologist and was recently elected to their parliament. Eliphilet (Eli) Miano went on to study civil engineering at Alberta, before returning to Kenya, where he set up a consultancy in civil and structural engineering. By their simple presence, these two men, along with the cadre of lively Irish grad students, helped give the otherwise bland campus a cosmopolitan feel.

The *Gauntlet* editor that year was John Macfarlane, later one of Canada's most successful publishers. John properly charged me with showboating when, to demonstrate our support for James Meredith's attempt to become the first African American admitted to the University of Mississippi, the Union proposed offering him admission to UAC. The idea was encouraged only by the folks down in Mississippi. In my desire to bring the issue home, I forgot to factor in logic.

My presidency completed, I was succeeded by Paul Unongo, a student from Nigeria. I was delighted by the news of his candidacy. Again, it would enhance our fledgling university's developing sense of maturity. But a friend of mine, Dave Surplis, was concerned both by Paul's lack of qualifications and by the possibility that he would be acclaimed simply because he was from abroad. Dave ran against him, but Paul won. Unfortunately, though, Paul proved somewhat authoritarian. Midway through the year his council voted him out of office and replaced him with the vice-president, Bill Sherriff. Paul later became a prominent (but still controversial) figure on the national political scene in Nigeria.

During my year as Union president, so that I and another English major, Mike Lapidge, could begin work on our MAs at UAC, several professors volunteered to teach grad courses for one or both of us. The rigorous writing demands — a major essay each week — prepared us well for our finishing year in Edmonton. Mike went on to earn an international reputation as an authority on Anglo-Saxon literature, holding senior appointments at Princeton and at Cambridge, where he retired.

To his credit, despite his difficulties with me on *The Gauntlet*, Principal Taylor was unfailingly cooperative during my term as student body president. When I ran into him a decade later in Toronto, he greeted me warmly and was pleased to find that I was now a professor at Brock University, in St. Catharines, Ontario. "I often use you as an example in my lectures on university management problems," he informed me cordially. I'm only sorry he didn't live longer than he did. No doubt he would have enjoyed hearing of my tribulations in university administration — although, as a dean, I was more often troubled with recalcitrant faculty than with obstreperous students.

I enjoyed writing my books. That's why I did them, certainly not to get rich. There's something captivating about telling a story. I daresay the telling can be as enchanting as the hearing. To pour oneself out like that — it's a real pleasure.

I suppose all my stories were somehow rooted in my life, in me. Of course, my actual experiences, especially in the war, are treated rather directly in my memoirs — *Winged*

Dagger, Operation Tombola. They are fictionalized somewhat in *The Day After Tomorrow.*

Come to think of it, I was rather touched when young Morris, from the paper, cropped up at a signing to buy the paperback of that one, when it came out. It was at Evelyn DeMille's bookshop, which was a marvelous addition to Calgary. Here, I told him, you don't have to buy that. I'll bring you a copy on Monday. No, he said, I want to. That was a nice gesture. I signed it, "To my friend and journalistic colleague." I wonder if he kept it.[25]

But even my works of fiction, the novels, inevitably draw on my life and nature. I hope that when people read *Jungle Chase*, for example, they pick up something of the colour and atmosphere that I found so intriguing in East Africa.

I don't pretend my novels are great literature. But I try to tell a story with enough flair and detail and drama that people can leave their own lives behind for a while and be swept into the book's.

And then I like to tuck in what I've learned. For example, the natives out there spike their homebrew, what they call *skokiaan*, with carbides — dead rats, rotting vegetables. Now, in the West, *skokiaan* is mainly just a nonsense word in a silly Hit Parade song from the fifties. I know better, so I explained what *skokiaan* really is. Any time you can dispel an illusion, that has to be worthwhile.

That bit of detail is hardly vital to the story, of course, but it gives the sense that in this fiction there is a lived life. And it reminds us what a different culture, what a different humanity, those natives have.

In *The Search*, the hero is a British veteran who flees a broken affair to become a farmhand in Alberta. *Mutatis mutandis*, that character has something of me in him, though his particular experiences — not just the broken affair — were certainly not mine.

But, as I look back, even in that story there's an attempt to break

through the racial or ethnic stereotypes that complicate our sense of
others, especially during and after
a war. Even as we try to see people
as individuals, often their behaviour
only reinforces the negative traits for
which they, as a group, are notorious. Stereotypes, alas, are often true.
In that book I illustrate that theme
through the brutish German character, but it could just as readily be ap-
plied to Russians, the Irish, Italians,
the Jews, the Arabs.

Though I didn't live the hero's experiences, that story does reflect my
knowledge of Alberta farm life. For
instance, the visceral feel of running
a milking machine, the difference between the European and the western
Canadian ways of stooking hay, that
sort of thing. And there is certainly
something very personal in my adul-
terous vagabond's revelation at the
end, that the truth for which we spend
our lives searching is God.

In *Never Had a Chance*, the girl's
Catholic faith sees her through to the

end — and it gives the young thug a taste of redemption, too. I guess there is a good deal of me in my stories. My fiction. That's inevitable.

After I left Calgary for grad school, my political differences with Roy only broadened. He had recoiled at the signs of my first beard and turtleneck. (I would have preferred black, but only the green was on sale.) I was metastasizing, first into a loathsome beatnik, then into a repugnant hippie. I got involved in the anti-war movement. He would rant against the pacifist "Lefties" in Hillhurst-Sunnyside.

I thought my old hero was — well, he was obsolete. The times had left him behind. Now, when I reread his conclusion to *Winged Dagger*, I felt embarrassed for him:

> I prayed to God for a meaning to these last eight years. If we had struggled in vain, if they had all died for nothing, and this were victory, I could see no good use to which I could put my freedom....
>
> Where was the meaning? With the Union Jack still flying over nearly one-fifth of the world's land surface, however much it is daily reduced, they say we are a bankrupt, third-rate Power.... With the country torn by bitter class-strife as never before, I asked myself if our leaders had stolen our soul....

> I asked myself if these people were wrong to put the world before Britain instead of putting Britain before the world. Can a nation have a soul if it is so selfless that it is ashamed to be patriotic? Oh, Lord, give us back the driving force of national pride.... Show me the way to use well my freedom and tell me that it has not all been in vain.[26]

I guess there is still a nobility in those lines. But it's an outdated nobility, archaic, with a whiff of gunpowder and mothballs.

Of course I sent Roy my books. For a while I was a poet.

The French are a melancholy people.
All their streets start with "rue."

He calls this poetry? Poetry is Kipling. This is silliness.

He probably likes that ridiculous Monty Python too. Nonsense.

Only after I became a professor did I fully come to appreciate my debt to Roy. He taught me skepticism and gave me an eye for substructure, for the unseen motives and relationships behind public utterances and systems. That was excellent preparation for the study first of literary texts and then of film.

He also made me write a lot, fast, precise, about everything, and when I wasn't writing, I was editing or proofing. Thanks to that training, I became a productive scholar, able to write quickly, easily, and with pleasure.

And something else. Roy Farran taught me the spirit of the maverick. As a second-year English major, I was swept away by Cardinal Newman's *The Idea of a University* and by John Stuart Mill's argument for the importance of solitary dissent against a mass opinion. My career, first as a teacher and critic, then as a university administrator, was most certainly shaped by the Roy Farran model — the lone voice against the tide.

With some differences, of course. I never risked my life.

Ah, Morris has a new book out! *Hitchcock's British Films*. Jolly good.

Well, let's see now. Hmmm...what the hell is he on about?...What is this? Analysis? Tommyrot, I would say. Pure tommyrot!

Hitchcock was an entertainer, not some airy philosopher. He made flicks! Damned good flicks. Let him be.

Roy was, by most accounts, a successful politician. In 1961 he was elected to Calgary's City Council and, for the next eight years, proved to be an effective alderman. As in his paper, he always defended the citizen.

Roy joined the Progressive Conservative party. Of course, in those days a self-respecting anti-Semite would have joined Social Credit — but, in any case, they had been too long in power. They were Authority.

In 1971 Roy was elected to the Alberta legislature in Peter Lougheed's upset win. After a typically heated campaign, Roy defeated the veteran Social Credit incumbent, Robert A. Simpson, and the brilliant New Democrat Barry Pashak, who later had a distinguished career as an MLA. As minister of telephones and utilities in the first Lougheed government, Roy updated the phone system, doing away with party lines. In 1973 he set up a new natural gas program, encouraging the formation of co-ops to buy at bulk rates.

Appointed solicitor general in Lougheed's second government, Roy increased funding for police forces and struck new initiatives in prison reform and the treatment of young offenders. Despite his own reputation for drinking, he also initiated the controversial breathalyzer program. In fact, Roy was one of the first Albertans to be charged and fined under it.

His share of the vote rose from 43.8 percent in 1971 to 71.2 percent in 1976. That was remarkable because Roy was not your typical Alberta politician. He sounded British, that is, intellectual. He never dropped a *g* in his life. He spoke seven languages, including Hebrew (which I don't). He wrote eight books.

Inevitably, though, the right-wing maverick went too far. Roy left the cabinet after breaking with its decorum. He was the only cabinet minister to state openly that, by mishandling evidence, the police had bungled an enquiry into a carnival company. He made national headlines with an off-the-cuff suggestion that hardcore convicts should be sent to work camps in the Arctic. When two provincial health care workers were accused of sexually assaulting juveniles, Roy lost his temper at a press grilling and accused the press of promoting sexual licence by condoning pornography.

Upon retiring from politics, Roy was appointed chair of the Alberta Racing Commission, a plum that paid $54,600 a year. With his usual hands-on zeal, Roy negotiated the conflicts between the thoroughbred side and the standard. He persuaded the government to give the racing community almost all the income from gambling, instead of the old 50-50 split. He also made Alberta's racing commission the first to ban steroids. But he lost his campaign against off-track and simulcast betting, and some people accused him of siding with the establishment by discouraging broader participation in horse racing. His full-time chairmanship ended after sixteen years with the part-time appointment of Doug Mitchell, former chair of the Canadian Football League.

Roy continued to be controversial in his columns in the *Herald* and the *Edmonton Journal* and on his CFAC talk show. In 1994, after he established a foundation in the Vosges Mountains for Franco-Canadian student exchanges, the Légion d'honneur joined his 1946 Croix de Guerre.

In addition to his official undertakings, Roy was a driving force behind the creation of the Nose Hill and Fish Creek parks. He held directorships on the boards of the Alliance Français, the Calgary Stampede, Calgary Hospital, the Fanning Care Centre, the Calgary Zoo, and the Calgary Winter Club. In 1962 Roy and Graham Smith together promoted Lynn Garrison's campaign to preserve a Lancaster FM-136 in Calgary. This anticipated the establishment of Calgary's military and aviation museums.

Very few Calgarians have left such a mark on the city.

* * *

The Rubovitz family could not forget their Alexander — or Roy Farran. In 1974, when one of Alexander's nephews, Moshe Rubovich (as his branch of the family spelled the name), was on a four-year posting as a teacher in the Toronto Hebrew Schools, he travelled to Calgary hoping to ask Farran where Alexander was buried. Mr. Rubovich could not get a meeting.

All that he managed was a snapshot of Mr. Farran riding at the head of the Calgary Stampede parade.

* * *

Me, I never did become a journalist. Not officially. For fifteen years, while I was teaching at Brock, I wrote four weekly TV and film review columns for the *St. Catharines Standard*. In a readers' poll I was edged out only by "Hints from Heloise." Advice about removing stains is undeniably more valuable counsel.

In 1995 my twenty-year digression into university administration brought me back to the University of Calgary. President Murray Fraser said he drew shocked laughter when he told alumni sessions at home and abroad that the notorious Poppy Day Yacowar had returned as dean of the Faculty of Fine Arts.

Back in Calgary, I phoned Roy Farran. My parents both dead, I guess I needed him to see what I'd become. To grant me his approval one last time. He didn't return my calls.

People said he was fine, still enjoying his horses — and his legendary drinking. Roy was already a dangerous drinker in his army days. Perhaps he had to be. There's a line in *Winged Dagger*, when he recalls the emptiness into which he awoke in London after v-e Day, surprised, disappointed perhaps, that he had outlived the war: "It was as if someone had blown out the last candle. Now I would have to make an effort to settle down or commit slow suicide as a heavy drinking, useless soldier."[27]

He knew the type. In Calgary he often drank after work with the *Herald* and *Albertan* reporters, who found him a soft touch. He was always good for an extra round. Alcoholism and journalism, they used to go together like tea and sympathy. And perhaps what Roy saw in the war left another thirst.

Well into his seventies Roy kept up his riding, with the Foothills Hunt, wearing the resplendent kit of the 3rd Hussars. He continued despite taking some horrendous falls. In his last race he was challenging the lead when his horse collapsed and died.

Roy also had I don't know how many near-fatal car crashes. His life on the civilian roads was as charmed as his career in battle. (There'd been a joke: being assigned to Roy's regiment was like taking out an insurance policy.) Even when he was solicitor general there were stories of his drunken mishaps and the kind of cover-ups he had made his journalistic name exposing.

But he was alive. Evidently to the surprise of some. In 1996 *The Times* apologized for wrongly referring, in its July 27th edition, to the late Major Farran.

I went to a Highlanders Ball expressly to meet him.

I'd heard how he'd leave Ruth home with the horses while he'd be out drinking and dancing up a storm.

"Mr. Farran, I'm Maurice Yacowar. You might remember me? I worked for you on the *North Hill News*?"

"Of course I do. You were one of our delivery boys. Best damned delivery boy we had, too."

"Actually, we worked together in the office."

"Of course, you took the pictures. You were an excellent photographer. You and that Walter Petrigo. Did you know Graham went back to school? At seventy-six, he's getting an MA in history. Isn't that something?"

"Yes, I'd like to see him. Anyway, I'm married now. This is my wife, Anne."

"I am very pleased to meet you, my dear. You are lovely. Take good care of...your husband. He's a remarkable photographer."

At least he pretended to remember me. That was Roy. Gallant to the end.

But then what could I expect? Roy lived a big life. He was a major player; I had a bit part. He had to mean so much more to me than I ever could to him.

❖ ❖ ❖

But wait. Maybe Roy's memory was sharper than I thought. If you allow for metaphor and subtext, there may be a correctness in his confusion.

On his first go, I'm his delivery boy, and his best at that. Well, I was. He hired me for certain purposes — to do odd jobs, to prove to the Jewish community that he would hire a Jew, whatever — and I delivered.

"You know, Morris," Graham once told me, "after you left we hired several cub reporters over the years. You were the only one who worked out." The kid delivered. So he was their best delivery boy. The brusque old soldier dissolves into poet.

On his second go, I'm the photographer, and an excellent one, in a league with Walter Petrigo. But, of course, I failed at my photography assignments. Even my one artsy shot was a mistake. It wasn't really — cricket. If Roy remembered me as his photographer, he was remembering me by my failure. People do that. It may be unjust, but we're defined by our failures.

How did the Bard put it? "The failures men have live after them. The good is often turd."

Something like that. Memory. The tricks it plays.

* * *

I didn't see Roy again until I attended Ruth's funeral. She died on June 17th, 2005, at the age of seventy-eight. By then cancer had taken his larynx — that damned Amphora Brown — so he was talking through a hole in his neck.

Roy had learned to press his throat while speaking

so that he could still be heard. He was still giving speeches. At his Remembrance Day address in 2004 there probably wasn't a dry eye in the house.

Now he sat against a wall like a raja receiving ambassadors. I could only imagine how bereft the loss of Ruth had left him. But he had steeled himself. Those hard blue eyes had watered to grey, but he still had his ramrod spine. I don't know that he had a bone in his body that hadn't at some point been broken, but his spine was a saber.

Again he made a show of remembering me and thanked me for coming. I gave way to the next supplicant.

Then he died. Cancer. At least he died at home. As if with his boots on.

And I missed his funeral.

* * *

Three years later, a book came out. *Major Farran's Hat,* by a highly accomplished professor of history at the University of London, David Cesarani. I read some reviews and heard a feature on the CBC. Cesarani asserted that Roy had tortured and then killed Alexander Rubovitz. Suddenly, my hero had feet of blood.

But maybe Cesarani was wrong. Or fabricating. Or — hey, I'm an academic. I have heard the sound of one axe grinding.

Then I read the book. The details, the citations: Cesarani makes a solid case. It's based on documents the British government had suppressed for sixty years. Nor is Cesarani alone. His revelations cohere with the earlier findings of University of New Brunswick professor David Charters as well as with those of a Brooklyn detective, Stephen Rambam, who is investigating Rubovitz's murder.[28]

I suppose everyone thought I'd done it.

But my men — not just my unit, but officers throughout the British army — they rallied behind me. They kicked in for my defence and flew the best solicitors that money could buy in from England. I dedicated my first book, *Winged Dagger*, to everyone who lent me money for that defence.

The court martial had to be held in Palestine. Any attempt to move it, anything that might look like a cover-up, that would have blown the international scandal even higher.

That bloody court martial. They had me by the short hairs, you know.

The thing is, I had been too damned

dutiful.[29] The morning after Rubovitz's death, I went smartly up to my commanding officer in the mess — that was Brigadier Bernard Fergusson — and I told him the whole story. Everything. I could have told him what I would later tell everyone else, but I couldn't. Honour, the military, man of my word, all that.

They found my hat at the scene of the abduction. That gray fedora, my name on the sweatband. F-A-R— something blurry, but maybe another R — then A-N. Took the poor buggers a while, but they eventually figured it out.

My commander did *his* duty and passed my report up the chain. Word gets around. Especially when the word could hang a man.

There was worse. When I was first arrested, I was told to write out what had transpired, as fully as I could remember. So I did. Just as I was told. As always. (Except when I didn't. Which was more usual.)

Then, like a fool, I left that written confession behind. It was saved. It was copied. It was going to be produced at my court martial.

Fortunately — for me — my lead solicitor, William Fearnley-Whittingstall, came up with two brilliant strategies.

First, the defence demanded that the army produce the written orders defining the duties of my special unit. Of course, the British government couldn't let the army do that. The orders would have proved that the government ran assassination squads, undermining their every diplomatic pretense.

There we had them by *their* curlies.

Second, my solicitors dealt with my two confessions. As my commanding officer, Fergusson couldn't be required to reveal what I'd told him the morning after the incident. Nor could his reports to those higher up be admitted as evidence. Because that, you see, is the same privilege an accused man shares with his solicitor in a civil trial. The commanding officer of a regiment is considered to be the legal counsel of all his men. That point established, my written confession was easily disqualified. What I'd written was in the nature of notes I'd been ordered to make for my commanding officer. Again, privileged evidence.

The government wouldn't allow the army to fight the second strategy, about inadmissible evidence, because they were too cowed by the first.

They all reckoned I was guilty. Everyone. But I was acquitted.

Now I don't know what to think. I'd always believed him. And now there are cracks. Why, even the title of his war memoir, *Winged Dagger,* is apparently wrong. It refers to the emblem on the Special Air Service cap. But the badge is actually a downward-pointing flaming sword, King Arthur's Excalibur. Some sloppy work by a Cairo tailor made it look like a winged dagger. During the war that misreading took hold and Roy perpetuated it in the title of his book.[30] He wasn't exactly making a mistake himself, but he was repeating a common misunderstanding. So he's not infallible. Yet I'd always believed him. Always defended him... If only I could talk to him. Not like when we worked together, but really talk to him.

* * *

"Mr. Farran. Nice to see you again. How are you? Oh, yeah. That's right. Sorry about that. Look, I was hoping you could help me out here. You know I've always had faith in you. But suddenly I feel like ... like that hapless laser in the *Road Runner* cartoons. Wile E. Coyote. I'm running full speed, but there's no ground under my feet."

"I don't know what you're talking about. Your life's a bloody cartoon now? Seems like rather a fall from your *Four Feathers*, what?"

"I read Cesarani's book — *Major Farran's Hat*. Was everything I thought about you wrong?"

"Precisely what did you think?"

"Look, when someone who killed a sixteen-year-old freedom fighter ruins a popular mayor's life over eighteen measly bags of cement, where is virtue?"

"But this is life, Morris, not some black-and-white Western. Bad and good, there are shades on both sides. And can't one go back and forth, from one side to the other? In your white-hatted Mayor Mackay, I exposed a red-handed villain. Your noble sixteen-year-old was involved in murdering British civilians as well as soldiers. I served the public good — in the army, in my newspaper, then in the government. A damned sight better than had I been hanged in '48, wouldn't you say?"

"But how could you champion individual freedom, like in your crazy campaign against the fascist threat of fluoridation, when you'd killed — how many people in Palestine? And all to protect the uniform of your faded empire!"

"If it takes a saint to do what's right, will anything ever get done? Whatever you say about me, the good things I did were still good."

"And your ward system. Did you promote it on principle, or was it just a way to launch your own political career?"

"Does it matter? It works. Try imagining Calgary today without it."

"And all your indignant rhetoric. Wasn't that really just the same rage that drove you to hate and to kill?"

"Tell me. Do you excuse those Jewish terrorists, the Stern Gang, for killing innocent women and children?"

"No, no, of course not. Those killings were motivated purely by politics — because the Stern Gang wanted to put pressure on Britain, to speed Israel's independence."

"But you defend Israel's bombings now, don't you?"

"Certainly. Because now Israel is fighting off her annihilation. Palestinian civilians die not because of Israel but because Hamas and Hezbollah use them as human shields. All their wars since 1948 have been caused only by the Palestinian refusal to let Israel exist."

"They've always refused that. I daresay they always will. But the point is, you're adapting an absolute value to fit a specific context. So did I. You're as outraged at Israeli losses as I was at Britain's. Civilian deaths were as regrettable, but also as inevitable, in my war as they are in yours."

"I just don't know. Where does all this leave me? I'm just the *schmuck* who served you."

"Maybe. Strikes me, though, you did very well for yourself as a result."

"Yes. But was the Calgary Jewish community right to be appalled that I was working for you? Did you figure you could use my trust and my ambition to improve your image?"

"Like you used me to improve yours? Or did you always omit your *North Hill News* experience from your résumé?"

"My résumé was never strong enough to let me omit anything. But now I can't help feeling that everything I did for you — duping Donna Mackay, embarrassing that "communist" pianist, churning out material for a paper that polished up your image, that made the bloodied soldier a model citizen, all my...what were they? Successes? Well, now they seem like my moral failures. Even my ability to write quickly, is it really something of value or just a matter of expedience? My headlong rush to complacency."

"I daresay it depends on what you're writing. Why spend a month on a "Gridiron Gossip"? Of course, a bit longer might have helped that Remembrance Day *schlemozzle*."

"So now you speak Yiddish?"

"The Devil cites scripture, remember? But don't be so hard on yourself. You were sixteen. But a broth of a boy."

"Yes, but not now. Now I wonder whether some part of me believed those terrible Roy Farran stories. I know I wanted the job, the glamour. And I was impressed — by your accent, by your aura of culture. But was I deliberately living a lie? After all, even your heroism was rooted in an outlaw violence. Clearly it at least bordered on psychopathology. So did I just *pretend* to myself not to believe those stories?"

"Don't ask me, Morris."

"Oh, for Christ's sake, my name is Maurice. Why can't you ever get it right?"

"Habits die harder than we do. In any case, you're evading your own question. What did you know, and why did you pretend not to know it? Sidestepping the issue isn't good journalism, Morris — and it's worse morality."

"Oh, come on. You're going to lecture me about morality? Besides, I'm 'all growed up' now. I hate your bitter, knee-jerk conservatism — yet I still crave your approval."

"Yes, I was rather touched by your...wilt...at the Highlanders Ball. Pathetic, really. What must your wife have thought?"

"Maybe I needed that lawyer's lecture on intellectual dishonesty."

"How would that have helped? Look, I'm sorry you haven't found your peace as I have found mine. Perhaps being a Catholic helped. We find forgiveness. So there's no Catholic Portnoy, is there? In any case, if you ever do write this all out — I don't know, perhaps a play, a novel, a remake of *Paradise Lost* — I have a title for you. *Moishe Agonistes*. Only you would be stronger *with* a haircut."

"Thanks a lot."

"Look, you were a good lad, Morris, I always said that. Too bad you had a Canadian education. Still, you worked hard. If you're tortured by the past, I'm sorry. But at this point there's not much I can do for you."

"You could confess."

"Even if I'm innocent?"

"I could use a bit of clarity."

"Not wisdom?"

So. I killed the boy.

As your Cesarani has it, we were cruising for pamphleteers, five of us, when we spotted him. It was at the intersection of Ushiskin and Keren Kayemet streets, in Rechavia. He had forty, maybe fifty names on him, all people in LEHI. That's Lohamei Ha-Herut b'Yisroel. Fighters for Israel's Freedom.

We desperately needed to crack it. I reckoned — the lad, hell, only sixteen, lean on him, he'd talk. Apply a little pressure, and he'd name those above him. We needed that. We drove him out of Jerusalem to open him up. To Jericho.

We were under pressure. Two days earlier, twenty-seven Jewish terrorists had been broken out of Acre, our most heavily guarded jail. That smarted.

But the boy wouldn't buckle. He grew defiant.

Nein, ich vill ear zoggen gornisht. Gornisht! Geht in der erd. Gei kacken in der vasser arhine. Chazzer'em. Gei fock yousell! [As they beat him, he sings Israel's national anthem, "Hatikvah."] *"Kol od ballei vav, penee-ee-ee-ee-mah / Nefesh yehudi homiyah —"* Agh! *"Ulfa' atei mizrach kadimah / Ayin letziyon tzofiyah / Od lo avdah tikvatenu."* [31]

I started to walk away. Suddenly, on some mad impulse, I picked up a rock, strode back to the boy, and bashed his brains in.

Some say I had a short fuse. But people who knew me knew better. I was known to stay calm, whatever the circumstance.

My men got rid of the body. I don't know how. Or where. I'm told some people say it was buried near Gethsemane, beside the church, but that's probably just an emotional attempt to identify the boy with Jesus. A more plausible suggestion is Wadi Qelt, the canyon in the Judean Wilderness, east of Jerusalem. But I don't know. I don't.

Of course I regret killing the lad. When the interrogation failed, I might have let him go. But how could I? We had upped the ante. We couldn't just let him go.

After all, there's only one thing worse than a dead torture victim. A living one. Besides, he was no cherry-cheeked delivery boy. Or idealistic cub reporter. He was an active member of a murderous underground. Given half a chance he would gladly have killed me.

In war, the line between the soldier and the civilian rarely stays clear. The Palestinian civilians that your modern Israel is killing might as well be wearing uniforms — most of them are in effect soldiers. And many Palestinian soldiers die in mufti.

Frankly, I never found killing easy. I got riled up easily enough, but killing always weighed on me.

You can be a good Catholic and also a good soldier. If you're going to live with yourself, you have to be. During the Crusades it was easy. The cross, the sword, they were one and the same. But now it's hard. When soldiers fight in civvies, you lose your old certainties. You kill someone, but you can't always know whether the killing is justified or not. You're constantly on the whisker between honour and necessity.

I remember once, out on a burial detail in 1940, we came across an

Italian tank. The entire crew had been decapitated by a single shell. We couldn't extract the bodies. So I laid a petrol trail to the fuel tank and lit it.

But before I did that I said a short prayer for forgiveness. Looking back, perhaps that doesn't make sense. The men were dead; their heads had been blown off. But I had to say that prayer first. That was 1940. I was very young.

I could have been hanged in 1948. And maybe I should have been. It might have appeased my conscience. But I wasn't. I went on to . . . well, I'm not a man to toot his own horn. I had a good life. I'm very proud of my children — Sally and Terry, my daughters, and my sons, Peter and David. I'm blessed to have been able to spend so much time with them. As for my own track record, I think I helped more people, did more good things, after 1948 than before.

I suppose you could define me by that one night in Jerusalem. But is that fair?

Even after the army, I always found ways to be a leader. In my newspapers, on City Council, in the legislature. I led those communities as I had my units in battle. But I have no illusions about that. Leadership by example is just an admirable way to disguise a base motive: the need to impress someone else, to gain the upper hand.[32]

I couldn't afford guilt over Rubovitz. I had to get on with life. Nor could I admit to killing him. Not if I wanted to continue my public service. Instead, I carried Alexander Rubovitz's corpse on my back for sixty bloody years. And suppose I hadn't. My name would have done it for me.

All I can hope is that the good Lord has placed that one impulsive action on one side, and, on the other, whatever good I have done since, and may have done before — and that the scale tilts in my favour. However slightly.

"For your sake, I guess I hope so too. But what about Rubovitz? What peace does he have?"

"Perhaps more than you think. A life snuffed too soon is always a tragedy. I know you know that, Morris. But think about his legacy. If he can look down on Israel today, he can see his life's mission marvelously fulfilled. The desert is a garden. In technology, medicine, science, the arts, the ragtag colony he fought for has become a modern civilization. No other nation in the region has such a model democracy, assuring its citizens freedom of speech, religion, life."

"Yes, but in very important ways Israel is still back where it was when he died. It's beset all around by threats to its very existence. The Jews were the world's pariah then. Remember, what radicalized those Jewish terrorists was the *Sturma* incident."

"I know. A Romanian ship loaded with some eight hundred Jewish refugees. Britain refused to save them so the ship sank; all drowned. That was horrible. It was 1942, right?"

"Yes. My birth year. And that was three years after FDR turned away the *St. Louis,* with almost a thousand Jewish refugees, all sent back to the concentration camps. Jews became terrorists when they saw nobody else would help them survive."

"That may be true. But that's no excuse for terrorism."

"It explains it, why it was felt necessary. Despair. Now the Jews are still the world's pariah. With the Arab nations threatening on all sides, the UN still condemns only Israel. The British press, the Left everywhere, they always blame Israel. The only difference is that with the Nazis, other nations wouldn't help save the Jews. With the Arabs, they won't let Israel defend herself. Same difference. Rubovitz won't find much satisfaction there."

"But surely that's the world's fault, not his. He did his best. He assuredly did not die in vain."

"Maybe not. But clearly he was killed in vain."

Now there's that Alexander Rubovitz Street, in Jerusalem. But no *North Hill News*. Nobody reads my books. Not a video game based on any of them.

Who knows? Maybe it was destiny. Perhaps Roy *Alexander* Farran had to meet and to kill *Alexander* Chaim Rubovitz. Consider, two Alexanders there, tossed together on a black Jerusalem street, worlds apart in culture, experience, desires. One is made great by his sacrifice, his death. Of course, that would be the Jew. The other, he is damned because — because he survives. And the more he makes of himself, the more he is damned. Just because he's had the nerve — yes, I know: the *chutz-pah* — to survive. The more successful and valuable his life, the more waste is found in the life he took.

No novelist would dare make that story up. Perhaps even that was like my court martial. It was all prearranged.

God holds all power. *Allahu akbar.*

Destiny. It's comforting — if you happen to be a coward. You can chalk anything up to destiny.

So there. I've confessed. I hope that makes things clearer.

Do you feel better now?

"Mr. Farran?"

"Yes?"

"I'm Maurice Yacowar? The lady in the front said I should come through? We have an appointment?"

Notes

1. Cesarani's book was first published in Great Britain, by William Heinemann, in February 2009 under the title *Major Farran's Hat: Murder, Scandal and Britain's War Against Jewish Terrorism, 1945–1948*. In April, Random House released a trade edition titled *Major Farran's Hat: Counter-terrorism, Murder and Cover-up in Palestine, 1946–47*. In the US, Da Capo Press published the book as *Major Farran's Hat: The Untold Story of the Struggle to Establish the Jewish State*.

2. Years later, after he had established himself as a minimalist cartoonist and writer, I ran into Ben in Toronto and gave him a ride. He told me that he used to do work for Roy out at his hobby farm in Midnapore and that Roy used the print-shop apprenticeship as an excuse, so that the paper would pay for his time. Then a separate town, Midnapore is now part of Calgary.

3. Until the advent of the Uptown, Calgary's classy cinemas were the Capital (where John worked), the Palace across the street,

and the Grand around the corner, all on the west side. But my world initially centred around the Strand, the Variety, and the Hitchin' Post—née the Empress—on 8th Avenue East. Johnny Cardell was the amiable manager of all three, working for the owners, the Leach family, one of whom continued as projectionist at the Hitchin' Post well into his seventies.

My chemistry lab partner, John Van Goor, was a bright, serious fellow who became a doctor. I lost touch with him after Central High, but he and another Central classmate-turned-doctor, Terry Groves, were especially generous in their medical treatment of my mother in her last years.

4. Yes, he was *that* Joe Clark, later prime minister of Canada. At university, I followed in Joe's footsteps as the holder of the R.L. King Memorial Scholarship in Journalism. The $250 was a lot of money at the time: a year's tuition. As for Roy's business, the contract printing would outlive the two newspapers. The *North Hill News* shop would be among six plants across the country contracted to print the *Globe and Mail*.

5. For Farran's version of the Rubovitz incident and his subsequent trial, see *Winged Dagger*, pp. 349–70.

6. Here, I'm again drawing on Farran's *Winged Dagger*, p. 370.

7. Ibid., p. 367.

8. Ibid., p. 239.

9. See Farran, *Operation Tombola*, p. 49.

10. For Farran's account, see *Winged Dagger*, pp. 370–71.

11. Calgary's discovery of civic corruption spread to Edmonton. There, Mayor William Hawrelak was busted for gross miscon-

duct, unseated, and forced to repay the Edmonton City Council $100,000. And after all that, he was re-elected.

As for Mackay, after failed initiatives in a jukebox company and a PR company, for which he again used his white-hat logo, he moved to Phoenix, where he tried to promote curling. In 1974 he returned to Calgary, was a sales representative for the Calgary Convention Centre, and then sold real estate. When he died of a stroke in 1979, aged sixty-four, his trademark white hat — his major legacy to Calgary — rode atop his coffin. The City of Calgary still bestows a white Stetson on important guests. Prince Philip once complained, on a repeat visit, that he'd already been given a hat: couldn't they think of something else to give him? He was, of course, duly criticized for his lack of the appropriate gratitude.

12. Farran, *The Search*, pp. 9–10.

13. Jim Finks came to the Stampeders in 1956 from a coaching job at Notre Dame. Over the next eight years, he turned our longtime losers into consistent winners by bringing in such players as Joe Kapp, Don Luzzi, Jack Gotta, Jim Bakhtiar, Bill McKenna, and Wayne Harris. In 1961, having secured "Eagle" Day, former Winnipeg Blue Bomber star quarterback, Finks negotiated a blockbuster trade that sent Joe Kapp to BC in exchange for four starters, headed by the defensive stalwart Ed "The Beast" O'Bradovich. In 1964, just as Wayne Harris was about to start playing for Calgary, Finks left to become the general manager of the Minnesota Vikings. Three years later, he launched the Viking dynasty, importing coach Bud Grant from Winnipeg and luring quarterback Kapp to Minnesota from BC. He later turned around two more football franchises, the Chicago Bears and the New Orleans Saints,

and was a successful president and chief executive officer of a baseball team, the Chicago Cubs. He died in 1994.

14. Farran's description of his Palestine experience is derived from *Winged Dagger*, pp. 343–50.

15. Ibid., p. 381.

16. This incident draws on Cesarani, *Major Farran's Hat*, pp. 193–96 and 201–2.

17. It was Ian Adam, together with my other mentors, Don Ray, Earl Guy, and Michael Taylor, who persuaded me to pursue an academic career in teaching. If I ever got better advice, I don't remember it. Both Birgitta Steene and I went on to publish on the films of Ingmar Bergman—she the first major book and I a very minor paper. But we never crossed paths again.

18. Roy Farran obituary, *The Times* (London), 6 June 2006.

19. Graham retired in 1981 and, in 1982, received a Bachelors of Education (with distinction) from the University of Calgary. In 1995, at the age of seventy-six, he earned an MA in history. He was also an avid camper and skier, cross-country and downhill, winning several medals in the Alberta Seniors Winter Games. An exceptionally fine man.

20. Much of the foregoing material derives from Cesarani, *Major Farran's Hat*. Farran also covers his early military career in the first chapters of *Winged Dagger*.

21. Cesarani, *Major Farran's Hat*, pp. 70–71.

22. Farran, *Operation Tombola*.

23. Farran, *Winged Dagger*, p. 341.

24. Cesarani, *Major Farran's Hat*, pp. 63–65.

25. The reflections that follow are my reading of Roy through his fiction, not his own. (And of course I kept the book.)

26. See *Winged Dagger*, pp. 382–83.

27. Quoted from *Winged Dagger*, p. 343.

28. See David A. Charters, "Special Operations in Counter-Insurgency: The Farran Case, Palestine, 1947," *Journal of the Royal United Services Institute for Defence Studies* (Great Britain) 124, no. 2 (1979): 56–61. Material pertaining to the court martial is available in the British National Archives, File WO 373/53/560.
    Stephen Rambam, of Pallorium Investigations, has reportedly been hired by an Israeli living in America.

29. From here on, Farran's description of the Rubovitz incident and trial is grounded in information drawn primarily from David Cesarani's *Major Farran's Hat*.

30. About the "winged dagger," see "Insignia" under the section headed "The Special Air Service" at www.echosquadron.com/aboutuksf.htm.

31. "No, I will tell you nothing. Nothing! Go to hell. Go shit in the sea. Pigs. Go fuck yourself!" The lines from "Hatikvah" ("The Hope") are: "As long as in my heart / A Jewish soul still yearns, / And on, towards the ends of the East, / An eye still looks toward Zion, / Our hope will not be lost." Rubovitz's words are my invention, but the report of the abduction and torture derives from *Major Farran's Hat*, pp. 95–99.

32. This paragraph was Roy. The rest here is my speculation.

𝔚orks by Roy Farran

Winged Dagger: Adventures on Special Services. London: Collins, 1948. Fontana edition, 1954.

Jungle Chase. London: Collins, 1951.

History of the Calgary Highlanders, 1921–54. Calgary: Bryant Press, 1954.

The Day After Tomorrow. London: William Collins, 1956. Panther edition, 1959.

The Search. London: Collins, 1958.

Operation Tombola. London: Collins, 1960. Special Forces Library edition, 1986.

Never Had a Chance. London: Geoffrey Bles, 1968.

The Wild Colonial Boy. Whitby, Yorkshire: Caedmon of Whitby, 1999.

About the Author

Maurice Yacowar is professor emeritus of English and film studies at the University of Calgary. Over the course of his academic career, he was Dean of Humanities at Brock University, where he helped found Canada's first degree program in film studies, Dean of Academic Affairs at the Emily Carr Institute of Art and Design, and Dean of Fine Arts at the University of Calgary.

His recent books are the satire *Mondays with Moishe* (lulu.com, 2009), *The Great Bratby*, a biography of the British painter (London: Middlesex University Press, 2008), *The Sopranos Season Seven* (lulu.com, 2007), *The Sopranos on the Couch: Analyzing TV's Greatest Series* (New York and London: Continuum, 2002; expanded editions, 2003, 2005, and 2006), and the novel *The Bold Testament* (Calgary: Bayeux Arts, 1999). He is also the author of *The Films of Paul Morrissey* (Cambridge and New York: Cambridge University Press, 1993), *Studies in International Cinema* (BC Open University telecourse, 1992), *Loser Take All: The Comic Art of Woody Allen* (New York: Frederick Ungar, 1979; expanded edition, New York and London: Continuum Press, 1991), *Method in Madness* (New York: St. Martin's Press, 1981; expanded edition, under the title *The Comic Art of Mel Brooks*, London: W.H. Allen, 1982), *I Found It at the Movies* (Brooklyn: Revisionist Press, 1978), *Tennessee Williams and Film* (New York: Frederick Ungar, 1977), *Hitchcock's British Films* (Nottingham: Shoestring Press, 1977; Detroit: Wayne State University Press, 2010), and *No Use Shutting the Door* (Fredericton: Fiddlehead Poetry Books, 1971). He provided the commentary for the Criterion laser disc editions of Paul Morrissey's *Blood for Dracula* (1996; DVD 1998) and *Flesh for Frankenstein* (1996; DVD 1998) and for Don Siegel's *Invasion of the Body Snatchers* (1987).

This book is set in Matthew Carter's Miller Display
and Jackson Burke's Trade Gothic, with the occasional
Goudy Text Cap.